GREAT AMERICANS
A PHOTOBIOGRAPHY

ELEANOR ROOSEVELT

IDEALS PUBLICATIONS INCORPORATED
NASHVILLE, TENNESSEE

COVER PHOTO: *Eleanor Roosevelt delivers a radio broadcast. Photo courtesy National Archives*

Editor, Nancy J. Skarmeas; Copy Editor, Michelle Prater Burke; Designer, Anne C. Lesemann; Electronic Prepress, Tina Wells Davenport

Copyright © 1997 by Ideals Publications Incorporated
535 Metroplex Drive, Suite 250
Nashville, Tennessee 37211

ISBN 0-8249-4079-2

Prepress by Precision Color Graphics, New Berlin, Wisconsin
Printed by RR Donnelley & Sons

Printed and bound in Mexico

First Edition
10 8 6 4 2 1 3 5 7 9

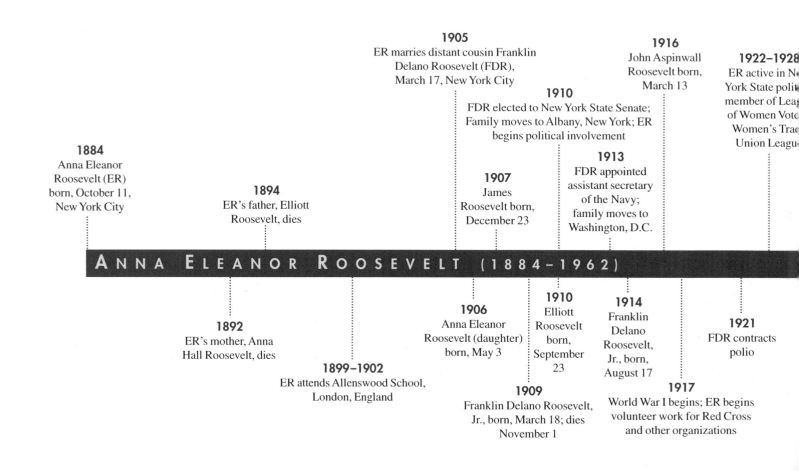

1884
Anna Eleanor Roosevelt (ER) born, October 11, New York City

1892
ER's mother, Anna Hall Roosevelt, dies

1894
ER's father, Elliott Roosevelt, dies

1899–1902
ER attends Allenswood School, London, England

1905
ER marries distant cousin Franklin Delano Roosevelt (FDR), March 17, New York City

1906
Anna Eleanor Roosevelt (daughter) born, May 3

1907
James Roosevelt born, December 23

1909
Franklin Delano Roosevelt, Jr., born, March 18; dies November 1

1910
FDR elected to New York State Senate; Family moves to Albany, New York; ER begins political involvement

1910
Elliott Roosevelt born, September 23

1913
FDR appointed assistant secretary of the Navy; family moves to Washington, D.C.

1914
Franklin Delano Roosevelt, Jr., born, August 17

1916
John Aspinwall Roosevelt born, March 13

1917
World War I begins; ER begins volunteer work for Red Cross and other organizations

1921
FDR contracts polio

1922–1928
ER active in New York State politics; member of League of Women Voters, Women's Trade Union League

ANNA ELEANOR ROOSEVELT (1884–1962)

P R E F A C E

E leanor Roosevelt lived a life without parallel or precedent, one which spanned seventy-eight tumultuous years of American history—two world wars, a devastating depression, the dawning of the nuclear age, the onset of the cold war, a revolution in the life of women, and the beginning of the American civil rights movement. She was a woman of action and of indefatigable spirit. Taught submission and dependence by the male-dominated culture of her youth, she chose instead a life of action and independence. Raised in an insular and exclusive class of American society, she rid herself of prejudice and embraced the world as her community. Eleanor Roosevelt never stood on the sidelines; she responded to the great many challenges of her life and times with an open mind, a generous heart, and a tireless commitment to service. What follows is not a traditional biography of this remarkable woman; it is rather a portrait drawn from a compilation of sources—a carefully assembled collection of essays, articles, editorials, letters, personal remembrances, and photographs that combine to describe the unique character and spirit of a truly great American.

"The influence you exert," Eleanor Roosevelt once wrote, "is through your own life and what you've become yourself"; to her mind, what mattered most in life was what one did to improve the world. By her own standards, then, Eleanor Roosevelt's life was an unqualified success. As the most popular, visible, and widely traveled first lady in American history, as a delegate to the United Nations, and as an international ambassador for peace and human rights, Eleanor Roosevelt touched and influenced lives in every corner of the world. Her story is one with which every American should be familiar, one in which each of us can find instruction and inspiration.

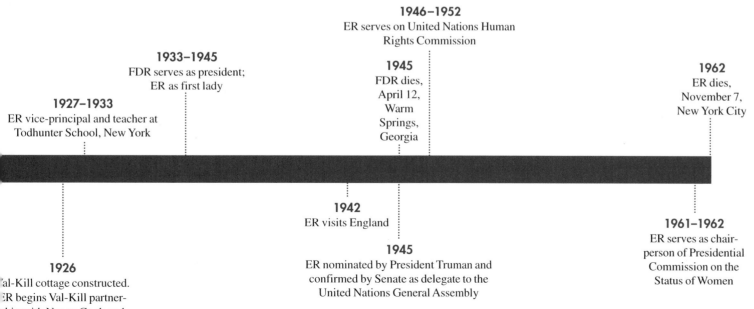

1946–1952
ER serves on United Nations Human
Rights Commission

1933–1945
FDR serves as president;
ER as first lady

1945
FDR dies,
April 12,
Warm
Springs,
Georgia

1962
ER dies,
November 7,
New York City

1927–1933
ER vice-principal and teacher at
Todhunter School, New York

1926
Val-Kill cottage constructed.
ER begins Val-Kill partnership with Nancy Cook and
Marion Dickerman

1942
ER visits England

1945
ER nominated by President Truman and
confirmed by Senate as delegate to the
United Nations General Assembly

1961–1962
ER serves as chairperson of Presidential
Commission on the
Status of Women

Eleanor Roosevelt
AT THE BEGINNING

BY HELEN GAHAGAN DOUGLAS

Eleanor Roosevelt wrote of her father, "He was the one great love of my life." Blessed with the infectious energy and spirit of the Roosevelt clan, Elliott was also cursed with a weakness for alcohol. Young Eleanor, however, saw only the bright side of her father—the man who loved her openly and uncondition-ally, quite in contrast to her often cold and disapproving mother. For years after her father's death, Eleanor fanta-sized about life with him; and throughout her life, his spirit, love, and devotion to her were among her most cher-ished memories. RIGHT: Eleanor and her father in April of 1889. Photo courtesy Franklin D. Roosevelt Library

At the beginning, the child Eleanor seemed to have everything: a distinguished family; wealth and position; a mother of great beauty; a gay, charming father who adored her; the companionship of two younger brothers. She had everything—everything, that is, except beauty.

Eleanor Roosevelt described herself as a painfully shy, solemn child. Her mother called her "granny" and seemed ashamed that she wasn't beautiful.

"Attention and admiration," she said in *This Is My Story,* "were the things through all my childhood which I wanted because I was made to feel so conscious of the fact that nothing about me would attract attention or bring me admiration."

She was not allowed to forget that she hadn't been given beauty. Little wonder that in her early years she wanted admiration and attention. This desire may also have been an expression of loneliness, of hunger. Hunger for the praise and approval of her beautiful mother; loneliness for the companionship of her beloved father, from whom she was mysteriously separated at the age of six. She didn't learn until she was a young woman that her father drank.

When she was eight, Eleanor Roosevelt lost her mother. She and her two brothers went to live with their Grandmother Hall. It was her mother's wish that their grandmother bring the children up. But her father's visits were the high point of her existence. Shortly after her mother's death, Eleanor's brother Elliott died, followed by her father with whom she had been "always perfectly happy." At ten, Eleanor and her brother Hall, to whom she was devoted, were orphans.

Grandmother Hall had welcomed them as her own children. They didn't lack care or discipline. Her grandmother, widowed early, thought that she had been overlenient with her own children. She was determined not to make the same mistake with her grandchildren. Mrs. Roosevelt described her childhood as one of nurses, rules, and regulations; mandatory formalities, manners, and codes.

Mrs. Roosevelt has told us that as a young girl she suffered from the stultifying effects of shyness.

Would Eleanor Roosevelt have had to struggle to overcome this tortuous shyness if she had grown up secure in the knowledge that she was a beautiful girl?

Eleanor Roosevelt's parents, Elliott Roosevelt and Anna Hall, were married in 1883 in what one New York newspaper described as "one of the most brilliant social events of the season." The marriage brought together two of New York's most prominent families and promised a prosperous union; Elliott, attractive and charming, and Anna, exceptionally beautiful and graceful, appeared perfectly matched. Yet the couple's surface similarities masked characters at odds: Anna was rigid and religious; Elliott effusive and lacking in self-discipline. The Roosevelts began their married life in a whirlwind of formal balls, travel, and yachting; but their marriage was soon in disrepair. By the time their first child, Anna Eleanor, was ten years old, both Anna and Elliott were deceased. LEFT: Anna Hall Roosevelt and Elliott Roosevelt. Photo courtesy Franklin D. Roosevelt Library

If she hadn't struggled so earnestly, would she have been so sensitive to the struggles of others?

Would a beautiful Eleanor Roosevelt have escaped from the confinements of the mid-Victorian drawing room society in which she was reared?

Would a beautiful Eleanor Roosevelt have wanted to escape? Would a beautiful Eleanor Roosevelt have had the same need to be, to do?

ALLENSWOOD AND MARIE SOUVESTRE

BY BLANCHE WIESEN COOK

In her will, Anna Hall Roosevelt named her mother, Mary Ludlow Hall, guardian of her three children, Eleanor, Hall, and Elliott, Jr. The children's father was still alive, but the family considered him too unreliable to take full charge of his children. From 1892 until 1899, when she sailed for London to enroll in a boarding school called Allenswood, Eleanor lived with her grandmother Hall, a strict, demanding woman of rigid principles. At her grandmother's, Eleanor had always imagined herself to be the outsider, the pitied orphan; at Allenswood, she was to find a new sense of belonging and self-worth. ABOVE: *Allenswood in late summer 1900. Eleanor is in the group to the right of the walkway standing near the door. Photo courtesy Franklin D. Roosevelt Library*

Though Eleanor was exposed to several gifted and learned teachers at Allenswood, Marie Souvestre was "far and away the most impressive and fascinating person." Physically she was "short and rather stout, and had snow-white hair. Her head was beautiful, with clear-cut, strong features, a very strong face and broad forehead." Her hair fell back in "natural waves to a twist at the back of her head. Her eyes looked through you, and she always knew more than she was told." For Eleanor, Allenswood was Marie Souvestre. And the best part of Allenswood were the moments spent informally in her company.

Like her Aunt Bye, ER became one of Marie Souvestre's intimate favorites. Perhaps it was, as Eleanor thought, because of Mademoiselle Souvestre's romance with America and Americans; or perhaps it was her keen ability to sense Eleanor's specialness. Whatever the reason, there was no doubt that, from her first week at Allenswood, she joined the innermost ring of Marie Souvestre's personal orbit. It was a place of unique privileges, and required special obligations. Eleanor Roosevelt delighted in every one.

Entirely bilingual, Eleanor was well prepared for the French-speaking school. At an advantage for the first time in her life, she thoroughly impressed her English schoolmates. One classmate, Helen Gifford, described Eleanor's first day during an interview with the London *Daily Mail* in 1942, when ER visited England: "I remember the day she arrived at the school, she was so very much more grown up than we were, and at her first meal, when we hardly dared to open our mouths, she sat opposite Mlle Souvestre chatting away in French. . . . "

At Allenswood, ER became confident in her abilities, and her personality flourished. A new maturity was reflected in her appearance. It was not just that she finally stood straighter. Now she claimed her full six-foot height, and walked tall with easy grace and pride. Mademoiselle Souvestre disliked Eleanor's hand-me-down and unflattering clothes and told her so. She encouraged Eleanor to use her allowance to have a long, really glamorous deep-red dress made by a Paris couturier. ER wore that dress with great pleasure every Sunday, and regularly for parties and school dances. No dress would ever satisfy her more. The tallest girl in her class, she was no longer gawky or ill-clad. And on a daily basis she looked very smart in the school's dapper uniform of long dark skirts, high-collared and occasionally ruffled shirts, striped ties, blazers, and boaters.

Her usual place at dinner beside Mademoiselle Souvestre had several advantages, among them the chance to share special dishes prepared for the headmistress and her party, and the chance to share in the exciting conversation that sparkled about her. There was an urgency to appear to know more than she in fact did, which she achieved by listening keenly to people's clever words, and appropriating them. But she lived in dread of being discovered, and continually made it her business to know more.

Eleanor had never before experienced female authority as a freeing rather than a constraining force. At Allenswood she was finally given permission to be herself, to act in behalf of her own needs and wants. Unlike her mother and her grandmother, Marie Souvestre encouraged direct inquiry, admired a free-ranging probing intelligence. Mannerly obedience, form without substance, mindless docility meant little, but rigorous thought was immediately rewarded, which meant that Eleanor was able to shine, to be noticed and admired. She was also given the opportunity to explore and express her own feelings. She was even allowed to cry in public, and she felt secure enough to have her very first temper tantrum. That was the greatest gift Marie Souvestre gave to Eleanor Roosevelt, the chance really to know herself—and her deepest emotions.

Physically, Eleanor was invigorated. Her chronic colds and coughs evaporated. Her frequent headaches disappeared. She began to sleep well, eat regularly with good appetite, and felt robust. Despite the cold damp English climate, ER wanted "to bear witness to the fact that I never spent healthier years. I cannot remember being ill for a day."

She played games and danced, enjoyed sports and competition. "One of the proudest moments of my life," she wrote, was the day she "made the first team" in field hockey. "I liked playing with a team and winning their approbation. It was a rough enough game, with many hard knocks." When ER made the first team and was cheered, she understood for the first time pure joy measured by personal success.

Eleanor Roosevelt was held in high esteem at Allenswood. Her presence and her opinions were sought after. She became, in fact, almost immediately the school's primary leader. Above all, she quickly created a circle of intimate friends who were among the brightest and boldest in her class, and who were acknowledged as Mademoiselle Souvestre's favorites. . . .

Classes were compulsory, and every hour was to be accounted for. There were "hours for practice, time for preparation—no idle moments were left for anyone." Exercise was also compulsory. A serious walk about the common after breakfast, in all weather—even when "the fog rose from the ground and penetrated the very marrow of your bones—but still we walked!" Although Mademoiselle Souvestre hated sports and could never understand "how girls could make such sights of themselves for a game of hockey," she required two hours of exercise after lunch every day. Then there was a four o'clock snack: "big slices of bread about half an inch thick, sometimes spread with raspberry jam, more often with plain butter." Then a study hour; then fifteen minutes in which to change for dinner.

Dinner at Allenswood was a formal affair. But in the evenings, "we worked again." Occasionally, however, "we were allowed to go down to the gym and dance." One afternoon a week was set aside for supervised mending, and there were occasional parties and outings. But for Eleanor the high points, the "red letter days," were those occasions when Mademoiselle Souvestre invited Eleanor and her friends to her study in the evening to read and talk.

Mademoiselle Souvestre's library, where she also held her classes, was a "very charming and comfortable room lined with books and filled with flowers." It looked out over "a wide expanse of lawn, where really beautiful trees gave shade in the summer, and formed good perches for the rooks and crows in winter." Filled with artwork, including the nudes of Puvis de Chavannes, which initially startled several of her students—Mademoiselle Souvestre's library was the site of ER's most splendid hours.

On most occasions, Mademoiselle Souvestre read aloud. ER recalled that she "had a great gift for reading aloud and she read to us, always in French, poems, plays, or stories." Her voice was "like Cordelia's," pitched "soft, gentle, and low." She might read a favorite poem two or three times and then "demanded that we recite them to her in turn." For ER that was a pleasure, since her memory was

No single experience shaped Eleanor Roosevelt's future as did her years at Allenswood. Located just outside of London in Wimbledon Common, the school was unusual for its day; at Allenswood, the young women of upper class European and American families were required to think independently and encouraged to imagine for themselves a life beyond the social sphere. ABOVE: ER's class at Allenswood, 1900. She is standing in the back row, third from right. Photo courtesy Franklin D. Roosevelt Library

well trained. But "others suffered to such an extent" that they froze, trembled, and "could hardly speak."

On other occasions, Mademoiselle Souvestre invited her favorite students to her study to proffer honors, or impart her views—messages she considered essential for this group of daughters of the leadership classes. She asked probing questions, exacted precise and thoughtful commentary, and evoked the best from those young women she judged special.

Mademoiselle Souvestre's library was the vital center for all the students of Allenswood. Every evening, they assembled there before going to bed. Mail was distributed, the roll was called, announcements were made. Then the students "passed before Mlle Souvestre and wished her good night." She had a word for each student, to encourage or to chastise. She either kissed you good night or took your hand. And, according to ER, her judgments were generally correct. "She had an eagle eye which penetrated right through to your backbone and she took in everything about you."

Marie Souvestre's legacy to her students was her own power—her clarity of vision, her personal vigor, and her deep learning. She demanded that her students take themselves seriously. She was often impatient, and she could be cruel. But she reserved her cruelty for students who failed to think, to apply their own understanding, convictions, and ideals to her lessons. A paper without reflection or independent thought might be torn apart in public.

ER excelled at writing papers. We "were expected to do a good deal of independent reading and research. . . and I labored hard over those papers." When she handed in slipshod work, it never went unnoticed. If criticized, she worked harder—rewrote, reconsidered, reflected more deeply. Eleanor enjoyed the process, and her work was generally acclaimed. Some of the others did not fare so well. Workaday efforts enraged Mademoiselle Souvestre. ER

Marie Souvestre, headmistress of Allenswood, was one of the great inspirational figures in the life of Eleanor Roosevelt. By respecting ER's character and intelligence, Souvestre prodded the teenager to greater efforts and achievements. Striking in appearance, outspoken, and often intimidating in manner, Souvestre taught ER to think for herself and to trust her instincts—skills that would later help her free herself from the restrictive, insular world of upper-class New York society and that would guide her throughout her adult life. LEFT: Marie Souvestre. Photo courtesy Franklin D. Roosevelt Library

noted, "I have seen her take a girl's paper and tear it in half in her disgust and anger at poor or shoddy work."

Mademoiselle Souvestre's explosive moods did not trouble Eleanor, whose years at Allenswood were entirely fearless: "For the first time in all my life all my fears left me."

From *Eleanor Roosevelt: Volume One 1884–1933* by Blanche Wiesen Cook, copyright © 1992 by Blanche Wiesen Cook. Used by permission of Viking Penguin, a division of Penguin Books USA Inc.

THE MOST UNEXPECTED DEVELOPMENTS

BY HELEN GAHAGAN DOUGLAS

Eleanor Roosevelt and Franklin Delano Roosevelt exchanged wedding vows in an Episcopal service on March 17, 1905, in New York City. ER's dress was covered with the same Brussels lace that had adorned her mother's wedding gown. She was given in marriage by her Uncle Ted—President Theodore Roosevelt—who had just weeks before taken the oath of office. The marriage rejoined the two branches of the Roosevelt family—Franklin's Hyde Park clan and ER's from Oyster Bay—that had diverged five generations earlier. ABOVE: ER's wedding portrait, taken January 20, 1905. Photo courtesy Franklin D. Roosevelt Library

Eleanor Roosevelt and her distant cousin, Franklin Delano Roosevelt, met in childhood but paid only passing notice to one another until the summer after ER's return from Allenswood. ER was working as a volunteer at the Rivington Street Settlement and Franklin was preparing for his senior year at Harvard when the two met by chance on a train outside New York City. ER was struck by her cousin's charm. Franklin, too, took a renewed interest: "She has a good mind," he remarked to his mother. ABOVE: ER and FDR at Campobello Island, August 1904. Photo courtesy Franklin D. Roosevelt Library

Eleanor and Franklin married despite the misgivings of his mother, Sara Delano Roosevelt, who protested that the couple were too young for such a serious commitment. Yet it was more than her son's age that troubled Sara Roosevelt; passionately devoted to her only son, Sara was reluctant to give him up to another woman. She needn't have worried; Sara remained the most influential woman in her son's life for years to come. LEFT: ER and her future mother-in-law at Campobello in 1904. Photo courtesy Franklin D. Roosevelt Library

That same year, 1903, was to bring the most unexpected developments. Eleanor Roosevelt, the most unlikely of the Roosevelt clan to make a good marriage, became engaged to Franklin Delano Roosevelt, the adored only child of Sara Delano Roosevelt. And when, finally, all the proper engagement formalities had been observed and all the prenuptial ceremonies completed, Eleanor Roosevelt was married, on her mother's birthday, to the young man considered the best catch in New York and Hudson River Valley society.

President Theodore Roosevelt (her Uncle Ted and her father's brother) gave the bride away. His daughter, "Princess Alice," was a bridesmaid.

After the honeymoon in Europe, Franklin and Eleanor Roosevelt began their life together.

But the young bride began marriage without "the faintest notion of what it meant to be either a wife or a mother." Eleanor Roosevelt was easy prey for the forceful, dominating woman whose only child she had married, and who was determined to continue to exercise authority and influence over her son's life.

It was Sara Delano Roosevelt who made the plans, who took the initiative. The bride found herself in almost the same situation in which she had lived as a child. She still deferred to an older woman. Sara Delano Roosevelt had taken the place of Grandmother Hall.

It was Mamma, as they called her, with the accent on the second syllable, who selected and furnished the house in which the young Roosevelts lived. It was Mamma who made it financially possible for her son and his young wife to live according to Delano-Roosevelt standards.

And not even motherhood—six babies in ten years: Anna, James, Franklin Delano, Jr. (who died in infancy), Elliott, Franklin, Jr., and John—changed Eleanor Roosevelt's subservient relationship to her mother-in-law.

It was Mamma who hired the stiff, starched English nannies whose attitudes were always condescending toward the mother of their young charges. It was Mamma's activities that set the daily pattern for the young bride's interests—Mamma's sewing circle, Mamma's daily drive. Eleanor Roosevelt never questioned Mamma's authority.

She was patient. She adapted herself to the requirements of her married life as she had to her grandmother's rules and regulations and as she would much later adjust to the demands of the White House.

From *The Eleanor Roosevelt We Remember* by Helen Gahagan Douglas. Copyright © 1963 and copyright renewed © 1991 by Hill and Wang, Inc. Reprinted by permission of Hill and Wang, a division of Farrar, Straus & Giroux, Inc.

[Nov. 24, 1903]   *Tuesday night*

Franklin dear,

I promised that this letter should be cheerier so I don't suppose I ought to write tonight for the day has been very trying. I wanted to tell you though that I did understand & that I don't know what I should have done all day if your letter had not come. Uncle Gracie's funeral is to be on Friday at ten. I have been twice to-day to Aunt Corinne's & I have promised to spend to-morrow morning there also. . . . The others have all gone to the play so I am all alone to-night as I would of course go nowhere this week, & I have been thinking & wishing that you were here. However, I know it is best for you not [to] come until Sunday & for me also as I should be a very dreary not to say a very weary companion just at present & there are so many things I know I ought to think of before I see you again. I am afraid so far I've only thought of myself & I don't seem to be able to do anything else just now.

Do you remember the verse I tried to recite to you last Sunday? I found it to-day & I am going to write it out for you, because it is in part what it all means to me:

> *Unless you can think when the song is done,*
> > *No other is left in the rhythm;*
> *Unless you can feel, when left by one,*
> > *That all men else go with him;*
> *Unless you can know, when upraised by his breath,*
> > *That your beauty itself wants proving;*
> *Unless you can swear, "For life, for death!"*
> > *Oh, fear to call it loving!*

> *Unless you can muse in a crowd all day*
> > *On the absent face that has fixed you;*
> *Unless you can love, as the angels may,*
> > *With the breath of heaven betwixt you;*
> *Unless you can dream that his faith is fast,*
> > *Through behooving & unbehooving;*
> *Unless you can die when the dream is past—*
> > *Oh, never call it loving!*

I wondered if it meant "for life, for death" to you at first but I know it does now. I do not know what to write. I cannot write what I want. I can only wait & long for Sunday when I shall tell you all I feel I cannot write.

Goodnight. I hope you will all have a very happy Thanksgiving at Fairhaven & please don't get tired out by working at night.

Always devotedly,

Eleanor

ELEANOR ROOSEVELT, POLITICAL WIFE

BY BLANCHE WIESEN COOK

After the election, Eleanor and Franklin went together to Albany to choose a congenial house. At 248 State Street they found a sunny, spacious, three-story place, with wide rooms, and so many of them that Eleanor decided to use only two floors. It was the first home they had to which Sara Delano Roosevelt came only as a guest, and she came infrequently. ER unpacked, established order and comfort, did her own marketing, and managed her own family entirely by herself. Neither Cousin Susie nor her mother-in-law was nearby to question her purchases or influence her routine.

ER's new freedom was as profound a change as FDR's decision to plunge into politics, and both involved her in an immediate choice: She could emerge from her depression and fulfill her lifelong wish to be really useful to someone she loved, or remain withdrawn and morose and be a terrible liability to her husband's new career. Her personal transformation into a woman of public affairs had begun that summer, as she contemplated and encouraged FDR's campaign from the isolation of Campobello. Geographically distant, she was enthusiastically involved in this new phase of her husband's life.

She experimented on every level, even before the move to Albany. Although she had breast-fed her other children, she now hired a wet nurse for Elliott, in the belief that baby Franklin might have lived had she been able to nurse him longer. ER's relationship with the wet nurse, a woman from Central Europe "who spoke no language known to us," reintroduced her to the ravages of poverty. ER felt "a great responsibility" toward the woman's own baby, visited the New York City tenement where she was boarded, and suffered "agonies" when she contemplated removing the infant's mother to Albany. Ultimately she could not do it:

The mother's suffering was unbearable. ER left the wet nurse behind, opened a bank account for her baby, and "kept in touch" for many years, until she disappeared. ER's ability to identify with that temporarily abandoned baby, and her mother—who "always seemed to me a defenseless person"—informed her perspective as she assumed her new role as a New York State politician's wife: "My conscience was very active in these days." She became immediately absorbed by the issues around her, as she recognized how deeply something within her "craved to be an individual. What kind of individual was still in the lap of the gods!"

For the new house in Albany, ER hired an entirely new staff. She dismissed the French nurse the children hated and replaced her with an English governess for Anna and James, and three efficient servants. Within twenty-four hours of her arrival on 1 January 1911, ER had the house settled; she also orchestrated and catered an Inaugural Day "open house" for as many of FDR's supporters, colleagues, friends, and constituents as cared to attend. For three hours on 2 January, the house was filled with revelers. And then it was cleaned. And then she unpacked, hung her photographs, and arranged all her ornaments. "I think it was my early training which made me painfully tidy. I want everything around me in its place. Dirt or disorder makes me positively uncomfortable!" After all that, she went to a dance at the home of the new Democratic governor, John Alden Dix.

The very next morning, she did all her marketing and began to meet her neighbors. Like Washington, Albany was a small, almost intimate political town. Everybody knew everybody; cautious friendliness was a way of life. Business was done everywhere—in the market, on the street, at meals, over coffee. It was the kind of life ER enjoyed, the kind of politics that came naturally to her. Within weeks, she had won the heart of virtually every political notable in town. She met their wives, talked with them easily, directly, and at length. She wrote Isabella: "We had 250 constituents to lunch on inauguration day . . . [and] since then I have met so many people that I feel quite bewildered and pay calls in every spare moment!" She had an amazing capacity to listen, to understand, and to care deeply. Even Tammanyites who considered Franklin a disloyal and stuffy prig quickly came to admire and like Eleanor. "I was to be very, very busy that year."

Eleanor Roosevelt would never be a society matron again. However proper and correct she might continue to appear when with Cousin Susie or her mother-in-law, or as other circumstances occasionally demanded, ER was now a political wife. She was involved in every step of the political game. People asked her why she did so much, and she said she did it all for Franklin. Nobody ever asked her if she enjoyed it. The fact is, from her first day in Albany she loved every minute of it.

Her renewed enthusiasm reinvigorated their marriage. From the beginning, ER had encouraged FDR's political ambitions. Unlike his mother, she understood that he would not have been satisfied with his father's country-squire routine; she knew that he deplored his days as a junior partner in a law firm, however prestigious. His entrance into politics saved them both from the kind of ordinary upper-class life, vapid and fatuous, that ER associated with society—at least that part of society where she had never felt welcome, comfortable, or understood.

Franklin's entrance into politics changed the family dynamics. Sara Delano Roosevelt's previously unchallenged power over her son and daughter-in-law began to be eclipsed. Their new concerns, those related to local and progressive politics, neither required nor interested her, and she rarely visited. Now that Sara was no longer so centrally involved in their lives, Eleanor began to take over those maternal duties that had been arrogated by Sara. Every afternoon was devoted to her children, ending with a children's tea before dinner, when she generally read to them, and she played with them after dinner.

ER patterned her entrance into the political arena on the example of her Aunt Bye. She met with people in their homes, and lobbied for causes. She encouraged debate and never avoided disagreement. Listening to all those conversations between her aunt and Uncle Theodore, ER had absorbed information, and style. FDR appreciated ER's opinions. He listened to her ideas, and trusted her insights about his colleagues. He appreciated from the first that she was one of his biggest political assets. She built bridges, even over the most treacherous terrain; she made what might have seemed impossible alliances.

Although ER dreaded speaking in public, she wanted FDR to become an appealing orator. She criticized his first efforts, which were slow and hesitant. He needed to sound both more assured and less arrogant. He needed to be more precise with facts, and more concerned about the real needs and wants of his constituents. FDR listened to his profoundly political wife as he listened to few others. It was she who went around and found out what his colleagues, and their wives, really thought. She went out among his constituents and talked with them, she attended Senate and Assembly debates regularly, and she reported on the subtleties and tricks lodged in every issue.

> "ELEANOR ROOSEVELT WOULD NEVER BE A SOCIETY MATRON AGAIN. HOWEVER PROPER AND CORRECT SHE MIGHT CONTINUE TO APPEAR WHEN WITH COUSIN SUSIE OR HER MOTHER-IN-LAW, OR AS OTHER CIRCUMSTANCES OCCASIONALLY DEMANDED, ER WAS NOW A POLITICAL WIFE. SHE WAS INVOLVED IN EVERY STEP OF THE POLITICAL GAME. PEOPLE ASKED HER WHY SHE DID SO MUCH, AND SHE SAID SHE DID IT ALL FOR FRANKLIN. NOBODY EVER ASKED HER IF SHE ENJOYED IT. THE FACT IS, FROM HER FIRST DAY IN ALBANY SHE LOVED EVERY MINUTE OF IT."

From *Eleanor Roosevelt: Volume One 1884–1933* by Blanche Wiesen Cook, copyright © 1992 by Blanche Wiesen Cook. Used by permission of Viking Penguin, a division of Penguin Books USA Inc.

ELEANOR ROOSEVELT
AND LOUIS HOWE

BY JOSEPH P. LASH

W hen the train reached Buffalo, Franklin went to speak in Jamestown, while Eleanor, with Louis Howe, decided to visit Niagara Falls, which she had never seen. This was a sign of their budding friendship. It had taken Eleanor a long time to appreciate Louis. At times she had resented his influence with her husband and had been swift to find fault with him. When Franklin went to Europe in 1918, she had complained that "the only item *every* paper gives is that Mr. Howe is running your office during your absence so he saw that was widespread news and how the naval officers must hate it!" But Howe was a sensitive, perceptive man who refused to be deterred by her coolness; he knew the blow she had been dealt by the Lucy

Bored with life as a New York City attorney, in 1910 Franklin Roosevelt ran for and won a seat in the New York State legislature. He, ER, and their growing family relocated to Albany, where ER began to emerge from the shadow of her mother-in-law and to forge a unique identity for herself outside the world of social calls, entertaining, and motherhood. She discovered an interest in social issues and public service and a talent for politics. The Roosevelt's Albany home became a center for progressive New York State politics, and ER and Franklin formed alliances that would last a lifetime. One such alliance was with Louis Howe, an Associated Press reporter who saw what he believed was great potential in Franklin Roosevelt. ER at first was repulsed by the chain-smoking, disheveled, unattractive Howe. But in 1920, when her husband was a candidate for the vice-presidency, Howe reached out to ER, who was feeling frustrated and excluded from her husband's campaign. Howe urged ER to get involved and convinced her that her presence and her opinions were of great value. By the end of the campaign, although Franklin was part of the losing ticket, ER had discovered a lifelong ally and true friend in Louis Howe. LEFT: ER, reporter Stanley Prenisol, Louis Howe, and FDR on the vice-presidential campaign train in 1920. Photo courtesy Franklin D. Roosevelt Library

Mercer business. She was the only woman on the *Westboro*, and he saw that many things bewildered or irritated her. At the end of the day Franklin would be tense and high-strung, and the men would gather at the end of the car to review the day's events, play a little poker, and hoist a few bourbons. Roosevelt "did not take life seriously enough," Steve Early, who was Roosevelt's advance man, later recalled. "He was just a playboy preferring poker to speech conferences." Eleanor disliked the playboy in her husband; she felt he should save his strength and go to bed, and that a candidate for vice-president should set an example.

She expressed her discontent obliquely; for example, she worried because she thought the car's porter was not able to get enough sleep because his berth was close to where the men played cards. She was timid with the newspapermen and wanted to be of more use than simply sitting with a rapt look listening to her husband make the same speech over and over again.

Louis sensed all of this: her loneliness, her great sadness, her lack of self-confidence, her need of appreciation. He was aware also of her abilities—her good judgment, remarkable vitality, and organizational gifts. He saw the way people responded to her warmth and courtesy. He began to tell her and she desperately needed to hear such words, that she had a real contribution to make to her husband's campaign. He brought drafts of speeches to discuss with her. He explained the ways of newspapermen and encouraged her to meet them as friends. By the end of the trip she was on good enough terms with the press to be amused rather than upset when from the rear of a hall, some of the reporters made funny faces at her to try to break the look of total absorption she adopted for her husband's speeches. They teased her when the ladies crowded around the candidate, and she took it good-naturedly. She was grateful to Louis for that. Together they discussed the issues of the campaign and the politics of the towns through which they traveled. Eleanor discovered that Louis had a wide range of knowledge, a nice sense of humor, a feeling for poetry and the countryside. Louis knew when to be silent and when to speak up. By the end of the trip they had become fast friends.

From *Eleanor and Franklin* by Joseph P. Lash, copyright © 1971 by Joseph P. Lash. Reprinted by permission of W. W. Norton & Company, Inc.

THE APPRENTICESHIP OF ELEANOR ROOSEVELT

BY DORIS KEARNS GOODWIN

The apprenticeship of Eleanor Roosevelt had begun with two remarkable League [of Women Voters] women, Elizabeth Read and Esther Lape. Read, an honors graduate of Smith College, was an accomplished lawyer; Lape, a Wellesley graduate, had taught English at Swarthmore and Barnard and then achieved prominence as a publicist. . . . Eleanor was immediately entranced by the stimulating lives these women led, with discussions of politics and public policy at dinner, and poetry readings after dessert. Their book-lined house in Greenwich Village reminded her of the happy days she had spent at Mademoiselle Souvestre's school in England.

When Eleanor first met Read and Lape, she was still suffering the effects of having discovered her husband's love affair with Lucy Mercer. She sorely lacked confidence. She needed appreciation and she was lonely. She found in Elizabeth and Esther's community of women the strength and encouragement to do things on her own, to explore her own talents, to become a person in her own right. Over the years, the friendships deepened into an intimacy which would continue for the rest of Eleanor's life.

Through her work with the League, Eleanor met two other lifelong friends, Nancy Cook and Marion Dickerman. Cook, a vital, tough-looking young woman, was the director of the Women's Division of the New York State Democratic Party. Dickerman, a tall, soft-spoken scholar whose grim countenance hid a dry wit, was a teacher and vice-principal at Todhunter, an exclusive girls' school in Manhattan. . . . Over the years, both women had been actively involved in the long struggle for women's suffrage, the movement to abolish child labor, and the efforts to establish maximum working hours.

There is every evidence that the four women, along with half a dozen others . . . played a substantial role in the education of Eleanor Roosevelt, tutoring her in politics, strategy, and public policy, encouraging her to open up emotionally, building her sense of confidence and self-esteem. In contrast to the distant relationship she had with most of the males in her life at this juncture, her relationship with her female friends was warm and open, frolicsome and relaxed. They kissed and hugged each other when they met; they had pillow fights at night; they wrote long and loving letters when they were apart; they challenged the traditional sense of what was possible.

When Eleanor first came into contact with these bold and successful women, she found herself in awe of the professional status they had acquired. "If I had to go out and earn my own living," she conceded, "I doubt if I'd even make a very good cleaning woman. I have no talents, no experience, no training for anything." But all this would change as Eleanor, encouraged by her friends, began to discover a range of abilities she never knew she had—remarkable organizing skills, superb judgment, practical insight, and astonishing endurance. In the space of two years, with the guidance of her female colleagues, Eleanor emerged as a major force in New York public life, speaking out in behalf of political reform, worker's rights, and children's issues, sought after for statements in newspapers, chosen to serve on all manner of committees. At the same time, she began teaching three days a week at Todhunter, organizing courses in literature, drama, and American history. "She loved it," Marion Dickerman recalled. "The girls worshiped her."

Though Franklin and Louis Howe sometimes joked about Eleanor's "squaws" and "she-men," they both recognized that she was becoming an excellent politician and that her tireless work around the state would inevitably rebound to Franklin's credit. Even before polio had crippled Franklin, Howe had encouraged Eleanor to become actively involved in politics. Once the polio struck, Eleanor's ability to stand in for her husband became critical. Moreover, both

Franklin and Louis genuinely liked Elizabeth and Esther, Nan and Marion, and found their conversation stimulating and absorbing.

For Sara, Eleanor's transformation was harder to accept. Sara was appalled at the idea of a well-bred woman's spending so much time away from home in the public eye. A woman's place was with her husband and her children. "My generation did not do those things," Sara explained. The more involved Eleanor became in politics, the less time she had to take Sara out to lunch or to pour tea for Sara's friends. "My mother-in-law was distressed and felt that I was not available, as I had been," Eleanor recalled.

Sara often displaced her criticisms onto Eleanor's friends, making them feel uncomfortable whenever they came to visit at Hyde Park, scanning their mannish suits and oxford shoes with disapproving eyes, glaring in bewilder-

ment at their close-cropped hair. To Sara, they all looked alike: unkempt, unconventional, unnatural. Understanding the situation, Franklin suggested that Eleanor and her friends Nan and Marion build a cottage for themselves in the woods so they could have a place of their own to pursue their interests apart from Sara's. "My Missus and some of her female political friends want to build a shack on a stream in the back woods," Franklin explained to Elliott Brown, whom he asked to supervise the project. He then became actively involved in the building of the "shack"—a fieldstone house which eventually grew to accommodate twenty-two rooms.

"The peace of it is divine," a grateful Eleanor told her husband the first summer she spent at Val-Kill, in 1925. From that time forward, though she stayed at the Big House whenever Franklin and the children were at Hyde Park, Val-Kill became Eleanor's home— the first home of her own she had ever had. "Can you tell me *why* Eleanor wants to go over to Val-Kill cottage to sleep every night?" a perplexed Sara once asked one of Eleanor's friends. "Why doesn't she sleep here? This is her home. She belongs here."

The woman who in 1925 had been frightened by the prospect of earning her own living was in 1941 among the highest paid lecturers in the country, pulling in $1,000 a lecture. Her syndicated column, "My Day," was printed in 135 newspapers, placing her on a par for circulation with Dorothy Thompson, Westbrook Pegler, and Raymond Clapper. And in 1938, the first installment of her autobiography, *This Is My Story,* had been published to widespread popular and critical acclaim.

In 1921, Franklin Roosevelt was stricken with infantile paralysis, or polio. The disease left him partially paralyzed and threatened to put a halt to his promising political career. Sara Delano Roosevelt urged her son to retire to their home in Hyde Park and live the life of a country gentleman. ER, however, threw herself into the task of helping her husband recover as much as he could physically and preparing him to re-enter the world of politics. Eleanor's desire to keep her husband's name alive in New York political circles dovetailed nicely with her own growing desire to be politically involved. In the 1920s, ER became active in the League of Women Voters, the New York State Democratic Party, and the Women's Trade Union League. By the time Franklin was well enough to return to public life, Eleanor stood on her own as a force to be reckoned with in the Democratic Party. ABOVE: A Democratic party meeting at ER's house in New York City in 1924. Photo courtesy Franklin D. Roosevelt Library

Reprinted by permission of Simon & Schuster from *No Ordinary Time* by Doris Kearns Goodwin. Copyright © 1994 by Doris Kearns Goodwin.

THE PEACE OF IT IS DIVINE

BY GEOFFREY C. WARD

There is nothing especially imposing about Val-Kill, Eleanor Roosevelt's retreat at Hyde Park. Visitors approach it along a bumpy lane that threads its way between woods and ragged fields, circles around a pond, crosses a noisy plank bridge, and ends in a grove of spindly pines. There are two main buildings on the property: a small, handsome fieldstone cottage, flanked by beds of flowers, which Franklin Roosevelt had built for his wife and two of her friends in 1925; and behind it, half-hidden at first among more substantial trees, an ungainly two-story gray stucco structure that still resembles the furniture factory it once was. That is where Mrs. Roosevelt lived for much of the last quarter century of her life; characteristically, when her partnership with her friends dissolved, it was she, not they, who moved into the converted factory.

Still, it is an evocative place, the only National Historic Site dedicated to the memory of a First Lady, and a monument both to a remarkable but troubled marriage and to its owner's determination to have a life and a home of her own.

The story of Eleanor Roosevelt's struggle for independence is much better known now than it was during her lifetime: she was far more than her crippled husband's "eyes and ears," and during their dozen years together in the White House she often acted as FDR's conscience as well, and sometimes as his goad, reminding him of the needs of people otherwise without access to him, while pursuing a host of political and social interests of her own. She set the standard against which every president's wife since has been measured, and after her husband died she became if anything more active, campaigning tirelessly for human rights and international cooperation—and for political candidates whom she believed would best carry forward the traditions of the New Deal. The title "First Lady of the World," which was inevitably conferred upon her during the final busy years of her life, may have been a little cloying, but it was also accurate; no woman was more universally admired.

Yet no matter where she went or what she was doing, she yearned to come back to this modest house and the woods and fields that surround it. "My heart is in the cottage," she once told a friend, and a glance back at her parched beginnings suggests why. Her father was Theodore Roosevelt's younger brother, Elliott, whose noisy disintegration preoccupied her beautiful but distracted mother. Even before she was orphaned at nine, she had been rootless, parceled out to relatives in a succession of exiles and abandonments which helped persuade her that she was somehow odd, unattractive, unable to count on anyone's love for long. At two and a half she asked her aunt, "Where is baby's home now?" and received no satisfying answer; there was none to give. At eighteen, she told another aunt, "I have no real home," and burst into tears.

Her marriage in 1905 to her buoyant fifth cousin Franklin seemed at first to promise just the sort of stability and support for which she longed, but, although the Roosevelts had six children over the next eleven years (five of whom lived), she never found in her husband a wholehearted emotional partner. He was unable even to provide her with a home of her own. Their first house in New York City had been rented and furnished for them by his fond but iron-willed mother, Sara Delano Roosevelt. In 1907, Sara had their second home built as a Christmas gift, then moved into its twin next door, connected with theirs by doors that were never locked. Summers were spent on Campobello Island, New Brunswick, in a cottage which stood just down the beach from hers. Even Springwood, the big comfortable old house at Hyde Park, in which FDR had been born and raised, and with which the public always associated him, was actually his for only the four years between his mother's death in 1941 and his own. It was still less his wife's: when the Roosevelts adjourned to its book-lined living room after dinner, FDR sat in one of the two massive carved chairs that flanked the fireplace, his mother in the other. "I sat anywhere," Eleanor recalled.

By the 1920's, the Roosevelts' relationship was more merger than marriage, an affectionate and hugely effective partnership based on a shared past and mutual interests but without passion or intimacy. Mrs. Roosevelt's discovery of her husband's romance with her social secretary during World War I, and her refusal ever to forgive him for it, had seen to that. And she had begun to carve out for herself in political and social work a career allied to his but independent of it as well.

Among the women she came to know and like were two who had lived and worked together for some years, Nancy Cook and Marion Dickerman. Miss Dickerman was tall and somewhat mournful-looking, an educator and social worker who had run for the New York legislature in 1919. Nancy Cook had been her campaign manager: she was short, sturdy, vigorous, and able to "do almost anything" with her hands, Mrs. Roosevelt wrote—jewelry, gardening, cabinetmaking.

Sometime in the summer of 1924, Franklin and Eleanor Roosevelt, Cook and Dickerman spread a picnic on the grassy bank of the Val-Kill, a cold clear stream about two miles east of Springwood, on land FDR had bought for himself. It was a lovely place and a beautiful day, and Mrs. Roosevelt lamented that this would be one of the last picnics of the year; her mother-in-law was soon to close the big house for the winter. FDR then suggested that the three women build a cottage on the spot: Cook and Dickerman could live there year-round if they liked, and his wife could join them whenever she wanted. He would give them a life interest in the land and supervise construction.

It was a generous gesture, but it also gave him an interesting project to oversee at a time when he had little else to occupy him other than his struggle to come back from infantile paralysis. "My Missus and some of her female political friends want to build a shack on a stream in the back woods," he wrote a contractor friend in the affectionately patronizing tone he sometimes used to discuss his wife's activities. The stream could be dammed to form a pond, and its water diverted to fill a pool in which he might exercise away from the claustrophobic solicitude of his mother. He signed on an architect, Henry Toombs, and told his wife, "If you three girls will just go away and leave us alone, Henry and I will build the cottage." They did, and on New Year's Day, 1926, it was officially inaugurated with a dinner party to which the whole Roosevelt family was invited; everyone, including Sara Delano Roosevelt, sat on kegs of nails.

"The peace of it is divine," Mrs. Roosevelt told her husband the first summer she spent there. She and her two friends all slept for a time in the same big dormitory-like bedroom upstairs, in a proximity that some visitors found startling; even their towels were embroidered with their intertwined initials. Life in the stone cottage in those early years had something of the air of Allenswood, the boarding school in England where Eleanor Roosevelt had spent three adolescent years, "the happiest years of my life."

Yet this was only the first of a series of extraordinarily fervent friendships Mrs. Roosevelt would form over the decades. The recipients of her devotion would eventually include not only Cook and Dickerman but the newspaperwoman Lorena Hickock, a genial strapping state trooper named Earl Miller—who was first her husband's and then her own bodyguard when FDR was governor of New York—Joseph Lash and his wife Trude, and in her later years her physician David Gurewitsch and his wife Edna. All would frequently visit Val-Kill and some would live there off and on. These men and women had little in common other than that there were ways in which Mrs. Roosevelt felt she could help them. Unable to attain the emotional support that she needed from her husband, she found satisfaction in gathering around her those whom she believed needed her.

In 1926, the three women built a furniture factory behind their cottage, intending to operate a successful business while helping local farmers and their sons stay on the land and earn a living during the lean winter months. Nancy Cook ran it, basing the designs for her bedsteads and trestle tables and bookcases on colonial models. Mrs. Roosevelt provided most of the financing and saw to the marketing, making the rounds of New York department stores herself, sample book in hand. . . .

The furniture business foundered, and in the spring of 1936 the factory was closed. Mrs. Roosevelt's friendship with her partners began to falter, too, for reasons never made entirely clear by anyone involved, and the following year she moved into the remodeled factory building. This was truly her own home and she eagerly saw to every detail of its furnishing. Her life at Val-Kill seemed almost consciously to mock the formality of her mother-in-law's establishment. The walls were knotty pine, the rugs laid down straight from the department store. "There wasn't a lamp that wasn't askew," a frequent visitor remembers, "and nobody cared if the cups and plates matched." There were framed pictures everywhere—103 in her sitting room alone—mostly photographs of friends and family.

"Tommy"—Malvina Thompson—her dedicated secretary, who devoted her life to working for Mrs. Roosevelt, lived in an apartment of her own in one wing of the first floor. Mrs. Roosevelt lived in another wing with a bedroom upstairs, but she spent all but the coldest nights on an adjoining sleeping porch where she could enjoy what she called the "peace of nature . . . healing and life-giving." She especially liked being snowed in on winter days, undisturbed except by the occasional creaking of a branch or the distant crackling of the ice in the brook; and every summer morning she watched from her bed as the sunrise was reflected in the still surface of her pond, its shore blanketed with purple loose-strife and punctuated by birch trees, their mirrored white trunks seeming to "reach down to the bottom."

Time for contemplation was rare, however, for Val-Kill soon became the social center for the Roosevelts whenever informality seemed in order. A large stone fireplace on the lawn permitted big cheerful picnics at which Mrs. Roosevelt happily presided, spooning out potato salad and grilling hot dogs for her husband's friends and for her own. (A smaller grill was placed next to FDR's chair on the lawn so that he could prepare his own steaks as blood-rare as he liked.)

Nancy Cook was an enthusiastic maker of home movies and her thousands of feet of jittery film provide an intimate record of life at Val-Kill during the gubernatorial and presidential years. One by one, the supporting players in the Roosevelts' vivid drama flicker past the camera. Tiny, wizened Louis Howe, already dying of a host of ailments, feebly tries to blow out all the candles on his birthday cake. Harry Hopkins, almost equally frail, capers barefoot within the President's outsize bathrobe. While someone holds the camera, Nancy Cook and Marion Dickerman skip rope girlishly in shirtwaists and long dark skirts. Sara Delano Roosevelt sips tea beneath a parasol, queenly and apparently serene even on her daughter-in-law's hard-won territory. Big Earl Miller, his handsome face split by a grin, his hair parted precisely in the center, strolls arm-in-arm with Mrs. Roosevelt, and later rides laughing alongside her through the snow, three police dogs barking silently at their horses' heels.

There are fleeting glimpses of FDR, too: performing childish hand tricks; playing water polo, his thin hair plastered flat, hurling the ball like a bullet; and seated on the edge of the pool in a dark bathing suit, teeth clenched around his cigarette holder, his enormous torso swollen to the point of caricature above his white, withered legs.

Although she treasured the peace of Val-Kill, Eleanor was rarely alone there. In addition to Marion Dickerman and Nancy Cook, with whom she shared the cottage, ER entertained a continuous flow of guests—friends, family, politicians, foreign dignitaries. Some, like her secretary Malvina Thompson, were almost permanent fixtures. LEFT: The exterior of Val-Kill. The window on the far left is in the dining room; at right is Malvina Thompson's screened porch. Photo courtesy Franklin D. Roosevelt Library

He died in 1945 at Warm Springs, Georgia. On the slow, sad trip north, Mrs. Roosevelt resolved to live out her widowhood at Val-Kill: ". . . it was mine," she wrote, "and I felt freer there than in the big house."

She planned a quiet life, working on behalf of her many causes but blessedly out of the Washington spotlight. "When I warn my friends that I am going to sit by a fire with a little lace cap and a shawl about my shoulders and knit baby things for the new generation," she wrote, "they look at me with some incredulity. The day will come, however, and when it does I think it will be rather pleasant." It never came. She could never stand to be idle, "could not bear to be alone," her last secretary, Maureen Corr, remembers.

"When you cease to make a contribution," she said at seventy-four, "you begin to die." She maintained a New York apartment so as to be near the United Nations and her other interests, and she actually accelerated the peripatetic travels she had begun as First Lady. Val-Kill was meant to be her retreat, a place to relax, but her notion of relaxation was different from anybody else's. She spent as much time there as she could, but surrounded whenever possible by friends and family. And after 1947, when Cook and Dickerman finally vacated the stone cottage and Mrs. Roosevelt's son John and his family moved in, there was always a full complement of grandchildren all summer as well, riding horses and boating in the pond. "Where Mrs. Roosevelt was, life flourished," Edna Gurewitsch remembers. "Dogs barked. The cook's grandchildren were being scolded. There was the smell of baking. Someone was diving into the pool. Something was *happening*."

Her guests were encouraged to rest while they were with her. She herself never wasted a moment. "I never saw her when she wasn't doing something," a friend remembers. She rose early to cut flowers so that when her guests arrived they would find in their rooms vases filled with varieties she knew they especially liked. Nearby were books she thought they might enjoy, along with bowls of favorite fruit or candy. She planned the day with Marge Entrup, her able and patient cook during her final years, who grew accustomed to having her employer tell her that she was at last growing old and would have to cut back on her entertaining; meanwhile, "Only fourteen for breakfast tomorrow, Marge."

She wrote down all her own checks, and balanced her checkbook, and she liked to shop, too, standing in the checkout line at the Grand Union or driving across the Hudson to a favorite farm in search of bargains. At least once a day she took a long walk in the woods with her dog, first her late husband's Fala and then with one or another of his boisterous Scottie successors, and in warm weather she plunged briefly into the pool, an activity she hated but thought "good for my character." And she found time to dictate her "My Day" column, write articles for books, brief herself for public appearances, and keep up with the mail that was delivered by the sackful. . . .

Christmas was the highlight of the Val-Kill year. Mrs. Roosevelt kept meticulous lists of all the gifts she had sent to scores of persons over the years so that she might never repeat herself, and she began Christmas shopping "about January the second," or so it seemed to Edna Gurewitsch. Items she had ordered by mail arrived almost daily during the spring and summer, and she brought others home from everywhere she traveled. The staff had orders to wrap them whenever they had a few moments to spare. Everything was in readiness by early autumn, a big upstairs closet no longer able to contain all the red and green packages.

In the early hours of Christmas morning, Mrs. Roosevelt padded silently along the corridors of her cottage, leaving stockings stuffed with sweets and small but skillfully chosen presents outside each guest's room. There were more gifts at each visitor's place at the dinner table. Mrs. Roosevelt offered her traditional toast—the same one she gave on the Fourth of July and Thanksgiving—"To the United States of America. To the president. To those we love who are not with us today." . . .

After dinner everyone filed into the living room, where there was a tree and the guests found their assigned chairs, each one heaped with still more gifts. Mrs. Roosevelt moved around the room as they were unwrapped, making sure that sweaters fit, toys pleased, books had not already been read. Her own gifts were left for last; one guest recalled that she liked best those things such as cheese or champagne which she could immediately share with others. She was firm about only one thing; paper and ribbon were to be saved and handed back to her to be used the following year.

Eleanor Roosevelt died in her New York apartment on November 7, 1962, at the age of seventy-eight. She had not wished to die at Val-Kill, she told friends, because to do so would have inconvenienced so many people who might have wished to come and see her. She was buried at the big house, in her mother-in-law's rose garden beside her husband as he had wished. A few weeks later, however, packages from Mrs. Roosevelt arrived in the mail for many of the friends and family members who had traditionally spent Christmas with her at Val-Kill. The gifts of course had been wrapped and ready since the summer.

From "'The Peace of It Is Divine': Eleanor Roosevelt" from *American Originals* by Geoffrey C. Ward. Copyright © 1991 by Geoffrey C. Ward. Reprinted by permission of HarperCollins Publishers, Inc.

TEACHING AND TODHUNTER

BY BLANCHE WIESEN COOK

Although Marion Dickerman, Nancy Cook, and ER co-owned Todhunter, and Marion was the principal, Eleanor's influence prevailed. She wrote the articles in magazines and school newsletters, raised the funds, attracted the students. Nancy Cook was largely involved with the Val-Kill furniture business, and appeared at Todhunter only occasionally. Marion Dickerman was very much present, but many of the students considered her less progressive, and rather less appealing, than ER. Both Annis Fuller Young . . . and Patricia Vaill . . . remembered Dickerman as dour, frosty, a traditional snob. There were other teachers at Todhunter—excellent instructors of art, music, geography, dramatics, languages, and athletics. But, like Marie Souvestre at Allenswood, ER eclipsed all others and dominated the landscape.

ER loved Todhunter. She loved young people. And she loved to teach. It gave her a forum for her vision and a new dimension of confidence and of real pleasure. That portion of her personal journey which she had begun at Allenswood in 1899 was resumed triumphantly at Todhunter. In 1930, she told a reporter that she meant to continue as a teacher, "because it is one thing that belongs to me." And in 1932, she told another reporter: "I like it better than anything else I do."

ER was a natural, enthusiastic, and exciting teacher. Her students adored her—she made them work, and she made them think. To Patricia Vaill, she made history and every character in it come alive—"And I never forgot a . . . thing she taught me." Every week, on the train to and from Albany, ER did her own homework. She read voraciously, prepared imaginative lesson plans, graded papers with long, thoughtful, sympathetic comments. Her message to her students was: Be Somebody. Be Yourself. Be All You Can Be.

As a teacher, ER consciously modeled herself after Marie Souvestre. Her own experiences with that great teacher caused her to believe profoundly that the main thing in education "is the interest aroused in a young mind by a stimulating, vivid personality." ER assigned her students research projects that would enable them to analyze controversial subjects from several perspectives, and to begin to develop their own points of view, their own theories about truth and fraud, decency and honor, morality and immorality—in politics, history, and private life.

As progressive as were some of Todhunter's educational methods, ER supported a traditional system of tests, midterm and final examinations, reports and grades. She and her colleagues believed, ER explained, "that the girls will have to take certain hurdles in life and that hurdles in school are an important preparation. We try, however, not to compare one child with another. And each girl plots a graph of her own term marks to demonstrate to herself whether she is gaining or losing."

ER's standards were high, and she was occasionally disappointed. Her senior girls were sometimes spoiled and

> "ER LOVED TODHUNTER.
>
> SHE LOVED YOUNG PEOPLE.
>
> AND SHE LOVED TO TEACH.
>
> IT GAVE HER A FORUM FOR HER VISION
>
> AND A NEW DIMENSION OF CONFIDENCE
>
> AND OF REAL PLEASURE."

indolent, sometimes impossibly unprepared. She wrote FDR on 2 February 1928, after her first semester at Todhunter: "I can't say I am set up by the exams my children did. I only flunked one but the others were none too good." Ever mindful of her own educational gaps as a young woman, ER was gentle but diligent.

She never forgot that dreadful moment of embarrassment during her honeymoon when she visited the Fergusons. Alone with Lady Helen at tea in the garden, surrounded by rhododendrons and tranquility, ER was "basking in contentment" until suddenly Lady Helen asked her to explain the structure of the U.S. government. ER repeated that story frequently, and as a teacher dedicated herself to several specific tasks: no student of hers would ever feel so unprepared or politically illiterate. More than that, she wanted her students to be as concerned about the great events of state and their solution as the finest spirits of England, like Lady Helen Ferguson: "a lovely and brilliant woman, typical of the alert Englishwoman who knows the politics of the hour to the latest detail."

All of ER's history and government students were prepared to answer a variety of questions on their final exams:

What is the difference between a citizen
 and a subject?

What is meant by a "public servant"?

List the ways in which your government
 touches your home.

Do you know of any way in which the
 government protects women and children?

How does the family income affect the
 standard of living?

What is the difference between civil and
 political liberty?

What is the object today of inheritance, income,
 and similar taxes?

Why is there a struggle between capital and labor?

Into what three different parts are our national
 and state governments divided?
 What is the function of each?

What is a tariff?

What is the World Court?

Who is Mahatma Ghandi?

Who is John Brown?

What were the causes of the Mexican War?

What was the Dred Scot case?

What were the causes of the Civil War?

How do you feel about the solution of
 the Indian problem in the Southern states
 during [Andrew] Jackson's term in office?

Give your reasons for or against allowing women
 to participate actively in the control of
 government politics and officials through the
 vote, as well as your reasons for or against
 women holding office in the government.

How are Negroes excluded from voting
 in the South?

Who is the dominant political figure in Soviet
 Russia?

Write an account of any article or series of
 articles on a subject you have read
 with most interest. . . .

ER's teaching methods were personal and informal. But, like Marie Souvestre, she held her students strictly accountable and suffered neither idlers nor parrots with notable patience. Although she did not encourage her students to become traitors to their class, she did promote responsible citizenship and urged her girls to challenge authority. "That is what the book says," she repeatedly admonished. "Now how would you put it?"

Above all, ER prepared her students to lead productive, cultured, and thoughtful lives: "Education only ends with death," she said repeatedly. Her own appetite for learning, for understanding the complexities and contradictions of the human spirit and society in all its forms, was what she sought to communicate. Less concerned with an isolated fact or date, she wanted to pass on to her students the tools they needed to make their lives an ongoing adventure in learning and understanding. For ER, the two primary tools were curiosity and vision.

After their March 1905 wedding, Eleanor and Franklin spent a week at Sara Delano Roosevelt's home at Hyde Park before returning to New York City where Franklin was to complete his law courses at Columbia University. That summer, his law degree complete, Franklin accompanied his bride on an extended honeymoon in Europe. LEFT: ER in Venice in July of 1905, photographed by her new husband. Photo courtesy Franklin D. Roosevelt Library

Despite the intellectual independence fostered in her at Allenswood, Eleanor followed family tradition and returned to New York City in 1902 to face the rigors of a very traditional society debut. RIGHT: ER at age eighteen. Photo courtesy Franklin D. Roosevelt Library

While on their honeymoon, Eleanor and Franklin visited family friends, the Fergusons, in Scotland. Lady Ferguson, like a great number of her Scottish contemporaries, was politically active and enjoyed discussing current events. ER was gravely embarrassed and disappointed in herself when she was unable to come up with a proper answer to Lady Ferguson's question about the workings of the American government. She vowed that day that she would never again display such ignorance. RIGHT: ER with the Fergusons in Scotland, August 1905. Photo courtesy Franklin D. Roosevelt Library

Franklin Delano Roosevelt was an energetic and robust young father who enjoyed roughhousing and sports with his children. Eleanor, in contrast, was restrained and formal. Only after Franklin was stricken by polio did Eleanor learn to enjoy relaxed, physical play with her children. ABOVE: FDR and son Elliott at Campobello in 1912. Photo courtesy National Archives

Eleanor Roosevelt

IN WITH THE RADICAL

BY CARL SFERRAZZA ANTHONY

It seemed that not a day passed during ER's tenure as first lady that she did not ruffle feathers and defy convention. When the controversial Workers Alliance offered the first lady honorary membership, she accepted, despite some public outcry. ER supported the efforts of the Workers Alliance to promote public awareness of the problems connected with rising unemployment. *ABOVE:* Three-year-old Irene Easley sleeps while her mother, Mrs. Hughs Easley, who was selected as "America's Unemployed Mother" by the Workers Alliance, dines with ER at a relief dinner on May 14, 1940. The first lady is eating a five-cent meal worked out by the Agricultural Department as typical of those which families on relief could afford. Mrs. Easley is eating a ten-cent meal, described as a "square meal." Photo by Associated Press/Wide World Photos

There was a tiny rosebud vase in Lou Hoover's Monroe Room that Eleanor accidentally broke as she lifted the delicate furniture out of the room to make way for her more durable Val-Kill factory pieces. While the chief usher was visibly startled to see a First Lady actually moving furniture, she was upset over the little vase incident, and secretively whispered the tale later to Cousin Alice. Eleanor had been worried that she had broken a delicate historic object. She had stared at the porcelain slivers a few moments. Then she swept them up and continued rearranging.

Alice teased her, "Out with the old, in with the radical!"

Eleanor gave directions as she took flight down the hall up the stairs—she disliked waiting for elevators—on her way to conferences, or in between dictation to her loyal personal secretary, Malvina "Tommy" Thompson, as she ran to catch a plane across the country, or a bus across town. Instead of taking the large First Lady's bedroom, she installed a narrow single bed in the dressing room, and used the grander room to work in while she was there. Which was not often.

When Franklin told her to stop worrying about not having cash on hand because he ordered a bank holiday as his first economic recovery move, she had an epiphany. She was now in a unique position during unique times. The intangible concept that clinical "New Deal" economists failed to grasp was the crippling malaise of spirit—something that could not be solved by a program. But Eleanor instinctively understood. When Louis Howe motored a timid First Lady over to the Bonus Army's camps, she didn't bring pension checks, just spirit. Lou Hoover had sent coffee and sandwiches from the safety of the White House; now, the First Lady was *in their camp*.

In all this was a paradox. What some saw as radicalism, Eleanor Roosevelt cherished as a traditional value—the noblesse oblige or duty of the affluent to serve those less fortunate. Whatever private tensions existed between Eleanor and Franklin, it was perfectly natural that they remained committed partners, helping each other help others. ". . . And those who are not employed will need more than they have needed before . . . and their courage is not as high as it was a year ago," Eleanor

On March 3, 1933, as America struggled to emerge from the Great Depression, newly elected president Franklin Delano Roosevelt delivered his first inaugural address, a speech, one White House observer wrote, so full of optimism and confidence that it renewed the "courage and hope and faith" of the American people. Twelve years later, Roosevelt delivered his fourth and final inaugural address. He told the small crowd that America must meet the test of World War II. "If we meet that test—successfully and honorably," he predicted, "we shall perform a service of historic importance which men and women and children will honor throughout all time." ABOVE: FDR delivers the inaugural address from the south porch of the White House on January 20, 1945. Photo courtesy National Archives

said over the radio in 1933. "So there is no reason for letting up in our sense of responsibility."

The severity of the Depression, the nature of her relationship with the president, and his dependence upon her to make his inspection tours all gave Eleanor Roosevelt the opportunity to break barriers. Having nearly two decades of professional experience with politics, organized labor, the press, rural issues, as well as careers in lecturing, teaching, and writing, she was superbly qualified to spur the changes she had long been spiritually motivated to make. Had the times been different, she might not have been able to expand the first ladyship to its limits.

Although admirers credited her with it, Eleanor hadn't consciously invented a "modern" first ladyship; it had been evolving. What she did was mobilize traditional components of a volunteer role into a "job," and though it may have sounded condescending to the ears of twentieth century activists, she was the modern Dolly Madison. First Ladies would no longer be judged against Mrs. Madison. The new ideal would be Mrs. Roosevelt.

"I truly believe," she said, "that I understand what faces the great masses of people in the country today. I have no illusions that anyone can change the world in a short time. . . . Yet I do believe that even a few people, who want to understand, to help, and to do the right thing for the great numbers of people instead of for the few can help."

She had never suffered from malnutrition or discrimination, never felt the terror of poverty, but Eleanor's experiences of psychological alienation and pangs of inferiority gave her a kinship with the neglected, and she instinctively saw the first ladyship as her springboard, a woman's version of the bully pulpit, as Uncle Ted had described the presidency. "I think in some of us there is an urge to do certain things and, if we did not do them, we would feel that we were not fulfilling the job which we had been given opportunities and talents to do."

From *First Ladies: The Saga of the Presidents' Wives and Their Power 1789–1961* by Carl Sferrazza Anthony, copyright © 1990 by Carl Sferrazza Anthony. Reprinted by permission of William Morrow & Co., Inc.

AMERICA'S MOST TRAVELED FIRST LADY

BY EMMA BUGBEE

A favorite cartoon of the Roosevelt years pictured a coal miner looking up from his work deep in a mine shaft and casually remarking upon the appearance of Eleanor Roosevelt. The cartoon was a tribute to the first lady's habit of turning up in the most unlikely places. During World War II, ER visited soldiers in England, Australia, on Guadalcanal Island, and in New Zealand. Admiral Halsey was originally reluctant to host the first lady's visit to the South Pacific, fearing that she would require special treatment at a time when the more pressing concerns of war deserved full attention. But Halsey saw firsthand how ER's presence affected morale as she toured hospitals, visiting every single bed in every ward. Her energy and spirit, and her genuine concern and kindness, lifted the sagging spirits of every soldier with whom she came in contact. Halsey called it "a sight I will never forget." LEFT: ER tours the Whakarewarewa thermal area in Rotorua, New Zealand. Photo courtesy National Archives

Mrs. Franklin D. Roosevelt enters upon her second year as mistress of the White House with energies undiminished and optimism unclouded. Already the most traveled First Lady in our history, with 40,000 miles to her credit in the twelve months since the inauguration, she piled up another 6,638 miles on her recent aerial dash to Puerto Rico. Returning to Washington, she at once picked up the threads of her many personal and public responsibilities without waste of motion.

The next few weeks will find her shuttling back and forth to New York as indefatigably as she did a year ago, when the nation, unaccustomed to First Ladies darting about, watched her with mingled admiration and alarm.

Today the admiration for her energy continues, but the alarm has been forgotten. It now is understood fairly well that activity of this sort does not fatigue the imperturbable niece of the strenuous T. R. She can pass hours in a train, hear great committees offer the freedom of a city, make a couple of speeches, eat a banquet meal, and return home on the midnight train, fresh as a daisy and ready to tackle several hundred letters, or stand beside her husband to shake hands with a thousand White House guests.

All of this, of course, is an old story to the newspaper women who described the activities of the President's wife in Washington and New York, but the Puerto Rico expedition massed much new evidence to strengthen the "Eleanor legend."

It showed us—even those of us who thought we knew her well—that thirteen days did no more than two or three to shake the perfect poise of the First Lady.

We flew with her, picnicked with her, watched her receive with equal grace the greetings of two Presidents of island republics and the prayerful benedictions of natives in calico and bandannas. We heard her wave away the protection of motorcycle police, native soldiery, mayors, and local reception committees, begging only to be allowed to make her serious investigations into island conditions as quickly as possible.

We followed her to the door of rickety thatched-roof cottages in the bamboo forests, where she knocked punctiliously on each door, asking, "Please may we come in and see your house?" We noticed that when she walked through the worst of the crowded alleys she was not afraid to wear, as usual, her rings and the monogrammed watch which was her husband's wedding gift.

When one of us stepped on a pig, reporter and pig squealed, and crowds laughed, but Mrs. Roosevelt's reaction was, "Poor thing."

We teased her a little, tho, when, at a certain landing, the supply of under-nourished children ran short, and her quick concern was aroused by a dog.

"Your dog looks rather thin," she was overheard to say to a welcoming official.

She traveled unofficially, like any other passenger, on the regular airplane from Miami to the West Indies. Whenever the airplane stopped for fuel, Mrs. Roosevelt strode down the dock, hopeful for her incognito, but determined to get air and exercise. Always there were roses, officials, Girl Scouts, and open-mouthed native children. The unofficial guest longed for a mantle of invisibility, but, failing that, she donned her mantle of official grace. . . .

We returned to Washington early on a Saturday afternoon, after thirteen breathless days. "The cocks crow us to bed and we breakfast under the stars," one of the company had written home. This was true—well, sometimes it was. It was true enough, at least, so that we all felt justified in calling it a trip and taking a day off.

But did Mrs. Roosevelt treat herself to a lazy weekend? Not that lady. . . .

In the next forty-eight hours she gave a wedding anniversary dinner, accompanied the President to church, welcomed her youngest son home from boarding school, entertained at the usual Saturday night chafing-dish supper, consulted with medical experts about her son's appendicitis, passed the entire Monday at the hospital when his operation was performed, and, that evening, laughed heartily at the gibes directed against her at the newspaper women's dinner, and responded in kind in the speech which ended the festivities. . . .

"No, I haven't had much rest," she laughed. "So much had accumulated while I was gone, and there was Johnny to visit at the hospital every day. But I feel perfectly fine."

No one need worry about a woman who carries on in such a fashion. Nor is it helpful to try to analyze this abundant serenity, which impresses those of us who study her most, as her greatest asset. More than any woman who ever lived in the White House she has succeeded in being herself despite its tabus.

It is no secret that, hating pretentiousness and formality, she had dreaded, for a while, her status as First Lady. But she just laughed at the tabus and they melted away. They told her no First Lady could drive her own car. She drove hers. They told her life would be one long procession of tea parties, and she hates "pink teas."

However, an abounding sense of humor and a complete absence of vanity put the protocol in its place. Now it and she live amicably together, but she really loves people and she loves helping good causes. The tea parties gave her opportunities for both. When you pin her down for a serious summary of her first year, you realize that she has a firm faith in the righteousness of the New Deal and that she has been deeply happy to share in establishing it.

"When you live in the White House," she says cheerily, "you cannot escape the public eye. All I ask is that when I run away now and then, it may be as a private citizen."

She seldom has her wish, for the American people must make a carnival around the First Lady. They peer at her in railroad cars and deposit roses at her hotel before breakfast.

Taxicab drivers in New York have ceased to be surprised when hailed by the President's wife, on foot and unescorted, on one of her frequent visits home. Keepers of gasoline stations up and down the Atlantic coast keep a wary eye out for the famous blue roadster. Last February, when the mercury hovered near zero in central New York, a filling station owner observed a car approaching with a District of Columbia license plate.

"Must be Mrs. Roosevelt. Nobody else would be driving up from Washington in this weather," he guessed—and guessed right. . . .

Thoroughly modern in her social philosophy, she almost never smokes and her light brown hair is unbobbed. (It also is untouched by gray, tho she is forty-nine years old.) She believes in the new education and the old religion. She is only a Right-Wing feminist. She utters New Deal preachments in pure Brahmin accents. She has not entirely escaped old New York, tho she looks forward to a kindlier social order. And she has no intention of relaxing her efforts to bring it about.

From *Literary Digest,* April 28, 1934.

ELEANOR ROOSEVELT CHARMS AS PUBLIC PRECEDENT BREAKER

AUTHOR UNKNOWN

"Dear God, please make Eleanor tired."

So runs the legendary prayer which reputedly falls from the trembling lips of the maids, secretaries, chauffeurs and Secret Service men who follow in the trail of America's First Lady.

But Anna Eleanor Roosevelt Roosevelt is tireless. She is the essence and symbol of that restless energy which, in less than two centuries, wrought the world's No. 1 nation out of wilderness.

This week, as she beams down upon the inaugural parade from behind the President's broad back, she will be embarking upon the most strenuous career any woman in the White House has ever had; embarking upon it with that priceless sense of humor which enables her to laugh at the tale of the child who, hearing the *Robinson Crusoe* saga, opined that the footprints on the desert isle must have been those of Mrs. Roosevelt.

Eleanor Roosevelt was leaving footprints long before her husband attained the goal of every American boy. The mother of six children (one died in infancy) is not apt to be idle.

When her husband became Assistant Secretary of the Navy during the Wilson administration, Mrs. Roosevelt took up war work in Washington, making sandwiches, ladling coffee, and handing out food to soldiers and sailors in troop trains at all hours of the day and night. . . .

When he was nominated for President, she continued as a busy and valued advisor to the Democratic National Committee. Having traveled more than 50,000 miles by plane, rail, and in her famous roadster during her first fifteen months in the White House, she soon became recognized as one of the major sources of the President's vast and detailed information about people and conditions in the United States.

Her defiance of precedent in a thousand ways was discussed all over the country, the first wave of opposition being succeeded by an appreciation of the value of her work for her husband and the people of the country. Always her sense of humor prevented her from being discouraged by criticism. She loved it when jokesters told about how Admiral Byrd set two places for supper in his South Pole shack, "just in case Mrs. Roosevelt should drop in."

Outstanding among broken precedents, begun by the President himself when he flew to Chicago to thank the Democratic delegates for his nomination to the highest office in the land, and carried on by the First Lady to defy convention are the following:

1. She is the first President's wife to continue her own career in the White House.

2. The first to hold regular press conferences.

3. The first to travel by air.

4. The first since the first Mrs. Roosevelt to serve food at receptions and punch at musicales.

5. The first to have traveled so widely, so extensively, and tirelessly, and to have examined conditions at first hand and under all situations.

6. The first to drive her own car on long trips and to refuse the guard of Secret Service.

7. The first to walk unrecognized among miners' wives in West Virginia and to descend into the mines in the regular cage for first-hand inspection of conditions.

8. The first to cross a dam (the Norris) in a cable car.

9. The first to drive over mountain trails (in Kentucky) and to win a walking marathon with reporters (Chicago Fair).

10. The first to wander as a tourist through San Francisco.

11. The first to announce with courage and with dignity that her son (Elliot) was seeking a divorce.

12. The first to make a fortune (for charity) by speaking. (In sixteen weekly radio talks of fifteen minutes each, Mrs. Roosevelt made $72,000, which she gave to the American Friends Service Committee for social work.)

13. The first to entertain girl textile workers (from Alabama) in the White House, and to give a garden party to inmates of a school for delinquent girls.

14. The first to edit a magazine (*Babies, Just Babies*).

15. The first to write a syndicated newspaper column, and to assist in the management of a furniture factory (Val-Kill).

To less ambitious mortals, what seems strangest of all is that the First Lady of the Land should choose to live like a human being; to maintain the privileges and pleasures of a private citizen. Never before has a President's wife engaged in so many activities, seen so many people of so many kinds, received and answered so many thousands of letters—or taken the stump for a friend.

Not for a long time was it known that she contributed her earnings to charity, and when it was leveled at her that she should harken to the wisdom of a woman's place being in the home, she retaliated . . . by saying that the conception of a home comprising only the four walls of a house was too outmoded.

But the domestic amenities of her home have been by no means neglected. She has taught women the world over that there is as graceful and dignified a way to scramble eggs for a Prime Minister (which she did for Ramsey MacDonald on March 24, 1934) as there is of advocating in a formal lecture the abolition of militaristic toys for children; that a woman can knit in the Senate Gallery with as much charm and composure as she can attend an Embassy or Legation tea in a simple street dress instead of elaborate afternoon attire (society women of Washington have learned from her that it is not ruinous to their reputations to wear the same

evening gown two seasons); and that there is a funny side to everything, even when one's youngest son comes home from school with twenty-two guests, and one has to prepare an unexpected supper for 100.

Mrs. Roosevelt is of vigorous intellect; her chief characteristic: unceasing seeking. "Go out and see for yourself," is her motto, "if you want to make other people feel what you have seen. The only thing to be afraid of is fear."

She says it convincingly, for she is convinced. When, through her guidance, her husband overcame fear during the early stages of his illness, his battle was won. "It is the battle of every individual; the battle of every nation."

The White House has known no hostess more gracious. The most coldly formal reception is made pleasurable by her presence. She is not beautiful, not even physically attractive in the opinion of many, but her every-day manner and conversation on any subject bear an ineffable charm that is completely winning. She has the rare faculty of making the White House seem, even to strangers, a real home. No guest has ever failed to feel the warmth of her abiding hospitality.

Alive, curious, seeking, actively humanitarian, pitying, sincere, Eleanor Roosevelt perfectly supplements the character of the man who is her husband. It would not be fair to say that without her he would be any less a great man, but it is possible to say sincerely that without her he might never have been President.

Eleanor Roosevelt traveled so much as first lady that a Washington newspaper once ran a headline reading "Mrs. Roosevelt Spends a Night at White House." To ER, travel was an invaluable means of keeping in touch with life outside Washington and the insular world of the White House. Her eagerness to see the world and reach out to people in every walk of life was an asset to FDR, who, due to his poor health, made infrequent trips outside the capital. The first lady looked upon her travels as a continuing education, and she returned from each trip eager to share that education with the president. ABOVE: ER delivers a message from the president to Naval personnel at the United States Naval Base in Brazil. Photo courtesy National Archives

From *Literary Digest*, January 23, 1937.

ENERGY: MRS. ROOSEVELT TELLS HOW SHE CONSERVES IT

BY S. J. WOOLF

Eleanor Roosevelt liked to deny that she possessed an inordinate amount of energy, yet she usually issued her denials as she ran out the door to make her next flight or appointment. ER believed that it was her obligation to explain her husband's policies to the people and to communicate the people's needs to the president. In her quest to do so, she covered an average of forty thousand miles a year during FDR's administration. LEFT: ER visits a women's refugee camp in Nagar, Pakistan, in 1952. Photo courtesy National Archives

Early next month the First Lady of the Land will be hostess to King George and the First Lady of the Empire. Mrs. Roosevelt is thoroughly familiar with the diplomatic etiquette that governs the visits of royalty to the capital, though pomp and circumstance mean little to her as an individual. So, while she will conform rigidly to protocol, her royal visitors will find an atmosphere of informality at the White House. Incidentally, they will discover a hostess endowed with astonishing energy and absorbing curiosity about things and people. No doubt the two sovereigns will have more than a glimpse of her wide range of interests.

How on earth, people are asking, does Mrs. Roosevelt find time to do so much? They look back over six years and recall some of her activities: talking over the radio; editing a magazine for a while; doing books and articles; conducting a daily newspaper column; and, of course, pursuing her duties as the wife of the President and as the mother of a large family, too—a family scattered to the four corners of a big country.

Seemingly, she has had to be in many places at once. In reality, she has just been in a lot of places in a very short time, by dint of being a fast traveler. She fires back, for instance, from a visit to a grandchild on the West Coast in order to greet an official visitor; then she hops off to deliver a lecture somewhere in the Middle West, or perhaps to visit a coal mine.

Six years ago, Mrs. Roosevelt bustled into the White House determined that her official position should not stop her from being herself. Some people laughed at the kind and number of things she did. Some people were shocked. That she should take part in a sponsored radio program seemed undignified to a number of her critics, even though the money she collected was given to charity. Their attitude did not deter her; she just went right on doing the things she wanted to do. And six years have seen a remarkable change in the country's appraisal of her. She has become a national figure in her own right and won the admiration of those who laughed at her and were frightened by her unusual ventures. By now they have sensed the sincerity and honesty of purpose behind everything she does. They have come to realize that she is motivated by an earnest desire to improve social conditions and that she has the happy faculty of being able to crowd into her day an amount of work that would wear out the average woman.

Dolly Madison is said to have saved the portrait of Washington when the White House was burned by cutting it out of its frame. Had Mrs. Roosevelt been in her place, she would have lifted frame and picture off the wall and carried them out of the flaming building. Then she would have sat down and written about the fire for the daily papers.

My appointment with Mrs. Roosevelt was for 3 o'clock and I arrived at the White House about ten minutes before that time. I sat talking in the main hall with Howell Crim, the chief usher, who said he was not sure in which one of the parlors Mrs. Roosevelt would pose. Portraits of Presidents Harding and Coolidge looked down austerely from their frames; the Presidential seal in brass glistened on the marble floor and liveried footmen moved noiselessly about. As 3 o'clock struck, Mr. Crim remarked it was strange that Mrs. Roosevelt was late.

Within two or three minutes a small car drove under the portico and stopped. Mrs. Roosevelt jumped out of the car and rushed into the hall, taking off her hat as she came and apologizing for being late. She asked me to go upstairs with her.

All formality was forgotten as this tall, lithe woman with a gracious smile entered. She brought with her an air of naturalness and hospitality which converted a cold public building into a home. When we had stepped into an automatic elevator, she did not wait for the hall man to push the button but did so herself.

At the second floor we got off and she led the way into a large sitting room in which the gloominess of heavy walnut furniture—it looked as if it had come down from the time of Grant and Hayes—was relieved by gay colored cretonnes. At one window sat a small kidney desk, such as any woman might use. She told me to make myself at home as she disappeared into an adjoining room to straighten her hair, which she said had just been set.

Before I had time to look at all of the photographs that lined the walls of the room she was back, explaining that while she could give me an hour to make my drawing, during the latter half she would have to dictate an article to her secretary, Miss Thompson.

"I do not know why people think I have so much energy," she said when I asked her how she managed all the things she did. "However, I will say that I am blessed with unusual health and that is a very important asset. But, in addition, I never worry about what is going to happen tomorrow. I may have a very busy day ahead of me but I forget about it until it comes around. Many people waste a tremendous amount of nerve force bothering about things that may happen in the future.

"Another great handicap is spending time regretting something that has gone wrong. When I make a mistake, naturally, I try to rectify it, but then I forget it and go to something else." I suppose the real reason why I can do so much is that I am tremendously interested in my work. Nobody can hope to accomplish anything who does not find joy in what he does.

"Of course," she continued, "I am fortunate in having a number of people to help me, people upon whom I can depend. Take my mail, for instance. The first year we were in the White House, I received 300,000 letters. It goes without saying that it would have been impossible for me to answer all of these myself. Miss Thompson, who has been with me for seventeen years, sifted them out and knew which ones should be brought to my personal attention.

"Last year, due to the fact that many people who had been in dire straits were being helped by the government, I did not receive so many. I think there were 90,000, but even that number was beyond me. So you see, a lot of my reputed energy is supplied by other people." . . .

Promptly at half-past three Miss Thompson appeared with her typewriter and Mrs. Roosevelt began her dictation. She dictates with great expression, as if she were talking to some particular person, stopping now and then not because she is at a loss for a word, but in order to give emphasis to what she has to say.

Suddenly, in the midst of the dictation, she stopped. Taking up her telephone from her desk she called someone downstairs and gave orders about what was to be served later in the afternoon.

The clock struck four and she got up. "I've got to go downstairs and greet 300 people," she said. "You wait with Miss Thompson." She rushed into her bedroom and within five minutes reappeared in a pink afternoon gown. "How do I look?" she asked as she darted for the elevator.

While she was gone Miss Thompson said that although a reception at the White House the night before had lasted until almost midnight, after it was over Mrs. Roosevelt had gone through all of the day's mail. Miss Thompson also said that she had never had one cross word with Mrs. Roosevelt in all the years she had worked for her; that Mrs. Roosevelt was always the same, never ruffled, never angry, always understanding.

Eleanor Roosevelt's humanitarianism knew no boundaries or borders; anyone in true need had an ally in the American first lady. ABOVE: A group of schoolchildren from Public School 169 in New York City presents the first lady with knitted garments to be distributed to the needy children of post-war Europe. Photo by New York Times Photos

Within a half hour the mistress of the White House returned. From a table she picked up a large wire basket filled with letters which she insisted on carrying over to her desk. There was to be another delegation, of 400 people, but she thought that she would have time to answer this part of her mail before they arrived. When my drawing was finished I left. As I stood outside the door waiting for the elevator I heard her dictating: "I wonder if it strikes you as it does me how remarkable it is that people can keep up their courage and struggle on in the face of so many hardships and if you feel as proud as I do of the high heart which so many men and women in our nation preserve."

Members of the press were fascinated by Eleanor Roosevelt; never before had a first lady been so informed, so vocal, and so influential. ER, in turn, appreciated the opportunity to communicate with the American people through the newspaper, magazine, and radio reporters that seemed to follow her everywhere she went. ER took a special interest in the nation's female press corps. While first lady, she held regular press conferences open only to female reporters, which gave many women journalists a chance they would not otherwise have received in a male-dominated field. ABOVE: ER talks to members of the press. Photo U.S. Navy, courtesy National Archives

Mrs. Roosevelt as a Political Force

BY D. W. BROGAN

In 1933, when FDR won election to his first term as president, ER did not relish the thought of leaving behind her active public life in New York and assuming what had always been a primarily social and ceremonial role. Of course, she transformed the role of first lady into one that fit her character: a position of activism, influence, and inspiration. While FDR's New Deal promised weary Americans relief from the Great Depression, ER developed her own set of complementary priorities: world peace; the abolition of poverty; equal rights for women, children, and minorities; and the establishment of the United Nations. LEFT: ER and FDR ride in an open car on Inauguration Day, January 20, 1941, marking the beginning of FDR's third term as president of the United States. Photo courtesy National Archives

Mrs. Roosevelt is among us; the Press is full, and rightly full, of comment on her terrific industry, her charm, her personal force, her work for women and children, her willingness to learn all about our social services and "how they have taken it," her representative role . . . as the most famous American woman, and so, in some respects, the representative of American women; all of these things we have heard about and should hear more about. But there is a side of Mrs. Roosevelt that is in danger of being neglected, if only because it is a side that cannot have any expression while she is among us. Mrs. Roosevelt is a great many things, but among others, she is a political force.

A political force, not a politician. Inevitably, as the niece of her uncle, the wife of her husband, Eleanor Roosevelt has been much exposed to politicians. She grew up under the shadow of one great politician, her uncle Theodore. She married an even greater politician. Hyde Park and the White House have seldom been without at least one specimen of the breed. And Mrs. Roosevelt has never pretended to be indifferent to politics, to be just a home-maker, just a wife, just a mother. But for all her interest in politics and politicians, she has not, in the ordinary sense of the term, been a politician. It may pain professional feminists to have to face the fact, but the woman, who, in American history, has played the greatest role in public affairs, has never run for office, never won the votes of others, and got her chance by being the wife of a master-politician. Women have had the vote for over twenty years. There is a woman in the Federal Cabinet; there are women in both houses of Congress; there are women judges; there are women holding other great political posts; but the woman who best justifies female emancipation is, above all, a wife, a mother and a grandmother.

But Mrs. Roosevelt could have been all these things without in any way representing the woman in public affairs. She could have been another Mrs. Coolidge or Mrs. Hoover. But she has not merely escaped from the White House and traveled nearly four hundred thousand miles, she has created for herself a political position all her own and has done it by not being a politician. When it became apparent, and it became apparent very soon, that the wife of the new President was not going to be just a White House chatelaine, or even a gracious mistress of a salon, but a personality in her own right, the regular party politicians were terrified. They were terrified of having to worry about what Mrs. Roosevelt said when they already had enough, they thought, of worrying what her husband did. Mrs. Roosevelt, in the early days, represented just the side of the new administration that the regular politicians disliked most. Washington was flooded with new faces, not merely new Democratic faces replacing almost identical old Republican faces, but new faces of a new type. Was there not a woman Secretary of Labour, in an office traditionally the perquisite of some tough, up-from-the-ranks, union official? Were there not college professors, men who had voted Republican or Progressive or Socialist, or had not voted at all, men who hardly knew their way to the Senate Office Building, all over the lot? . . .

It took the politicians some time . . . to realize that ordinary political rules did not apply to the Roosevelts, less even to Eleanor than to FDR. They began to think that, however distressing it might be to admit it, she was an asset. The women didn't dislike her as much as the wire-pullers had feared; the men didn't resent her as they should. Indeed, more than once, it was apparent that the President's wife, far from being a parasite on her husband's popularity and prestige, was able to lend him, at low moments, some of the political capital she had accumulated. "How come?" the politicians asked themselves, and they gave various answers, but they admitted the fact. The answer is not, in fact, very far to seek. . . .

In all the kaleidoscope of Washington and the United States, Mrs. Roosevelt stood still. Not physically, of course—few people have ever travelled as much—but morally and intellectually. For her, the New Deal was not just an experiment, a rag-bag of expedients; it was a chance to get into the American system some of the social conquests of less fortunate countries. In the expressive American term, Mrs. Roosevelt had a concern for the "underprivileged," and she did not conceal her preoccupation. She talked and she wrote. Often what she said in lectures and interviews, as well as what she wrote in her column, *My Day*, was trivial; but in every week's or month's stint of trivia or of banalities there was always to be found some solid, "indiscreet" comment on human wrongs, human sufferings, human disabilities, all of which Mrs. Roosevelt thought could be diminished by political action. And as she moved all over the country, winning friends and influencing people by her candour, her courage, her competence, she became a serious political force, an embodied League of Women Voters. Of all her assets, courage was the most striking. Mrs. Roosevelt was forever disdaining the human prudence of the politician to which her husband as President and as Head of the Democratic Party had to pay some deference. Mrs. Roosevelt paid none. . . .

For all the social aims and achievements of the New Deal, Mrs. Roosevelt is a campaigner and for her fellow workers a symbol. The politicians, the real politicians, no longer sneer, although they may grumble. I have once or twice made the experiment of suggesting possible presidential names to various practical politicians of the "get out the vote school." All of the male New Dealers leave them cold. "Couldn't carry his own precinct" is a fairly standard comment. "But, then, who have you got for 1944 or whenever FDR finally retires? What about Mrs. Roosevelt?" And there has more than once come into the computing eyes of these statesmen a look that is not hope, not fear, but rather speculative wonder. I don't expect Mrs. Roosevelt to enter the White House in her own right, but odder things have happened—not much odder, perhaps, but odder all the same.

And if it ever came about, it would be because Mrs. Roosevelt has never played politics or for her own hand. No wonder the regulars do not know what to make of her any more than "nice" people did or, perhaps, do.

VISIT TO ENGLAND

BY ELEANOR ROOSEVELT

"Every soldier I see is a friend from home," Eleanor Roosevelt wrote in her newspaper column describing her visits to servicemen and women in England in 1942. The soldiers returned her devotion, often remarking that a visit from the first lady was as comforting as a visit from their own mother. ABOVE: ER visits a motor transport school training British women in October of 1942. Photo courtesy Franklin D. Roosevelt Library

Every time Mr. Churchill came to the White House, he spoke of the time when my husband would visit Great Britain, but one felt that he had in mind a visit to celebrate a victory either in sight or actually achieved. I do not think it ever occurred to him that there was any good reason why I should go to Great Britain during the war. He assumed, I think, that I would go in my proper capacity as a wife when my husband went.

However, it evidently occurred to Queen Elizabeth, for Franklin received some tentative inquiries about whether I would be interested in going over and seeing the role that the British women were playing in the war. Naturally the British looked upon my visit as providing an opportunity to get that story told in the United States, for the queen, knowing I wrote a column and made speeches fairly frequently, felt, I think, that I had access to the people.

When my husband asked me how I would feel about going, I assured him that if he thought it might be helpful, I should be delighted to go. Knowing that the North African invasion was coming off soon, he said that in addition to observing the work of the British women, he wanted me to visit some of our servicemen and take them a message from him. As I have said before, I had always been sorry that, because of having young children, I had not been able to do any active war work overseas during the First World War. . . .

The trip to Great Britain seemed to offer me a chance to do something that might be useful. At once I asked Tommy if she would be willing to go with me, since I did not want to obligate her to take a trip that might entail some risk. She was entirely willing and gave as little thought to the possible danger as I did. I suppose the saving fact for all human beings at such times is that they never think anything is going to happen to them until it actually happens. Theoretically and intellectually they recognize the possibility, but in my own case, at least, it was not a sign of courage that I went ahead and did certain things which might have had some slight danger attached to them. It was simply that, like most human beings, I am not given to seeing myself disappear off the face of the earth. If it should happen, having no choice, I would, I hope, accept the inevitable philosophically.

After my husband told Harry Hopkins that I was willing to go (for I think Harry made the suggestion first), I received a formal invitation. I went ahead and made reservations on a commercial plane. I paid for our passage and was given instructions about the amount of baggage allowed, had the necessary shots, and on October 21 appeared at the airport on Long Island at the appointed time, together with Colonel Oveta Hobby, head of the Women's Army Corps, Lieutenant Betty Bandel, her aide, a courier from the State Department, and Mr. Slater, one of the vice-presidents of the American Export Lines. It was a nonstop flight, one of the first to be made. We were luxuriously taken care of and had only one piece of excitement on the way, when we were allowed to look down on a convoy below us—little tiny specks on the ocean. It was hard to believe that those ships were in danger and that some of them might suddenly be torpedoed. . . .

I had been worried by the thought of having to visit at Buckingham Palace, but I finally told myself that one can live through any strange experience for two days. I was determined, even though I had certainly not been asked to come on the trip to enjoy myself, to try to live each moment aware of its special interest. Though certain situations might be unfamiliar and give me a feeling of inadequacy and of not knowing the proper way to behave, still I would do my best and not worry. Nevertheless, as we neared London I grew more and more nervous and wondered why on earth I had ever let myself be inveigled into coming on this trip. I had to be treated as a "Very Important Person" because my husband was President of the United States.

Finally we pulled into the station. The red carpet was unrolled and the station master and the head guard on the train, both of them looking grand enough to be high officials of the government, told me that the moment to get off had arrived. There stood the king and queen and all our high military officials. The only person in the whole group whom I felt I really knew was Stella Reading. I evidently concealed my nervousness, because later Tommy told me that it was only my poise and calm that kept her from having the jitters.

After the formal greetings, the king and queen took me in their car, while Tommy was taken in hand by the lady-in-waiting and two gentlemen from the royal household, and we drove off to Buckingham Palace.

The king and queen treated me with the greatest kindness. The feeling I had had about them during their visit to the United States—that they were simply a young and charming couple, who would have to undergo some very difficult experiences—began to come back to me, intensified by the realization that they now had been through these experiences and were anxious to tell me about them. In all my contacts with them I have gained the greatest respect for both the king and queen. I haven't always agreed with the ideas expressed to me by the king on international subjects, but the fact that both of them are doing an extraordinarily outstanding job for their people in the most trying times stands out when you are with them, and you admire their character and their devotion to duty.

When we arrived at the Palace they took me to my rooms, explaining that I could have only a small fire in my

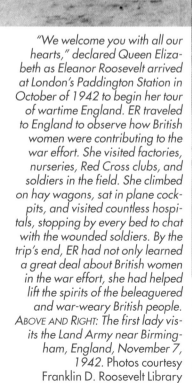

"We welcome you with all our hearts," declared Queen Elizabeth as Eleanor Roosevelt arrived at London's Paddington Station in October of 1942 to begin her tour of wartime England. ER traveled to England to observe how British women were contributing to the war effort. She visited factories, nurseries, Red Cross clubs, and soldiers in the field. She climbed on hay wagons, sat in plane cockpits, and visited countless hospitals, stopping by every bed to chat with the wounded soldiers. By the trip's end, ER had not only learned a great deal about British women in the war effort, she had helped lift the spirits of the beleaguered and war-weary British people. *ABOVE AND RIGHT:* The first lady visits the Land Army near Birmingham, England, November 7, 1942. Photos courtesy Franklin D. Roosevelt Library

sitting room and one in the outer waiting room, and saying they hoped I would not be too cold. Through the windows they pointed out the shell holes. The window panes in my room had all been broken and replaced with wood and isinglass and one or two small panes of glass. Later the queen showed me where a bomb had dropped right through the king's rooms, destroying both his rooms and hers. They explained the various layers of curtains which had to be kept closed when the lights were on; informed me that there would be a messenger outside my door to take me to the drawing room at the proper hour for dinner, and then left me to my own devices.

Buckingham Palace seemed perfectly enormous to me. The suite I had was so huge that when Elliot saw it he said that after this I would have to take the long corridor at the White House for my bedroom, because the one I had would never again seem adequate. The wardrobes were wonderful—the kind one longs for at home—but the fifty-five-pound limits on baggage made my few clothes look pathetic hanging in those wardrobes. I wondered what the maid thought when she unpacked them. One evening dress, two day dresses, one suit and a few blouses, one pair of day shoes and one pair of evening shoes comprised my wardrobe for a visit to Buckingham Palace! One of the

newspaper women, for want of something better to write about, later reported that I had worn the soles of my one pair of shoes through. The head usher at the White House read the story and very thoughtfully sent me another pair.

Everything in Great Britain was done as one would expect it to be. The restrictions on heat and water and food were observed as carefully in the royal household as in any other home in England. There was a plainly marked black line in my bathtub above which I was not supposed to run the water. We were served on gold and silver plates, but our bread was the same kind of war bread every other family had to eat, and, except for the fact that occasionally game from one of the royal preserves appeared on the table, nothing was served in the way of food that was not served in any of the war canteens.

With the king and queen I had my first real look at the devastation—blocks upon blocks of rubble. Our first stop was at St. Paul's Cathedral, partly because the king and queen wanted to give the faithful

watchers who had saved the cathedral the satisfaction of a visit from them at that time, and partly so that I could stand on the steps and see what modern warfare could do to a great city.

We drove for miles through the poorer sections of the city, from which the people had been evacuated. Some of the streets were literally lined with shell holes, and wherever I looked there was nothing but devastation. When we drove into the City we went through the usual ceremony in which the lord mayor meets the king and allows him to enter—an old custom which still survives in spite of war. I was struck by the amount of destruction in the City, but in spite of the evidences of bombing all around us we had tea with the lord Mayor, in the true British fashion.

I spent a weekend at "Chequers," the country estate given by Lord Lee to the British government for the use of British prime ministers. There I watched Prime Minister Churchill playing a game on the floor with his grandson and noticed the extraordinary resemblance between the two. Mr. Churchill once remarked that his grandson didn't look like him, he just looked like all babies. I recollect that at breakfast the following morning, the prime minister was displeased with what was on the table, feeling that it spoke of England's hardships.

Mrs. Churchill is a very attractive, young-looking and charming person. One feels that, being in public life, she has had to assume a role and that the role is now a part of her, but one wonders what she is like underneath. She is very careful not to voice any opinions publicly or to be associated with any political organizations. This I felt was true of the wives of all the public officials whom I met in England. As I have seen more of Mrs. Churchill over the years, my admiration and affection for her have grown. She has had no easy role to play in life, but she has played it with dignity and charm. . . .

With Mrs. Churchill I went to visit a maternity hospital, and also to see how the women in the several branches of the military service were trained. During one of those visits, I remember, the air-raid warning sounded, but the girls went right on with what they were doing and paid no attention. I saw girls learning to service every kind of truck and motor car and to drive every type of vehicle; I even saw girls in gun crews, helping the men to load the guns. I visited factories in which women did every kind of work, and I visited one group of girls whose job it was to fly planes from one part of the country to another. Since it was unwise to keep a concentration of planes anywhere in Great Britain, these girls would take over the plane when a pilot landed and fly it either to a place where it would be well camouflaged or to a repair shop. . . .

During this visit to England I started the practice, which I continued on subsequent trips, of collecting from the boys to whom I talked the names and addresses of their families, so that I could write to them on my return to the United States. I had quite a collection before I was through.

This was a nation at war, going through moments of great uncertainty and stress. But what I have often marveled at has been the people's staunchness and their ability to carry on during the years after the war and to accept the drabness of their life. I should not marvel, however, for in spite of all that had happened to them, I knew then as I talked to them that they would go on living and working for their country. The answers to many questions were in the faces of almost any crowd of Scottish and English people.

One of the workers with whom I talked told me that the hardest thing was to keep on at your job when you knew the bombs were falling in the area of your home and you did not know whether you would find your home and family still there at the end of your day's or night's work. When we lunched with some of the women who were daily feeding the dock-workers, they told me: "We used to look down on the dock-workers as the roughest element in our community. We were a little afraid of them; but now we have come to know them and will never feel that way again."

Women from many different backgrounds, who had never worked together before, were working side by side. These British Isles, which we always regarded as class-conscious, as a place where people were so nearly frozen in their classes that they rarely moved from one to another, became welded together by the war into a closely-knit community in which many of the old distinctions lost their point and from which new values emerged.

There was an old couple who still slept nightly in an underground shelter in London, though they could easily have been evacuated to a country area. They told me they had lived for so long in the shelter that, while they liked to go out in the daytime and sit in their old home—even though there was not enough of it left so that they could sleep there—they preferred to return to the shelter at night rather than to move away.

When I visited a center where bombed-out people were getting clothes and furniture and other supplies, one young woman with a child in her arms and another dragging at the skirt said to me very cheerfully: "Oh, yes, this is the third time we have been bombed out, but the government gives us a bit of help and you people in America send us clothes. We get along and none of us was hurt and that's the main thing."

ER's trip to England was met favorably by the British and American press. In fact, Joseph Goebbels, Hitler's chief of propaganda, hoping to protect the morale of the German troops and citizens, issued an order instructing German journalists to downplay the first lady's visit. To the British women working in the war effort, the American first lady, who was eager to learn from their experiences, was a true inspiration. LEFT: ER speaks with women in a motor-pool school in England in 1942. Photo courtesy Franklin D. Roosevelt Library

Eleanor Roosevelt gave little thought to her personal safety during wartime as she flew, drove, and sailed her way to the nickname "First Lady of the World." Her near-constant travel gave her security personnel fits, but to ER it was just part and parcel of the job of first lady. LEFT: ER visits the front lines at a Dover, England, bomb shelter in caves under the White Cliffs on the English coast. She is accompanied by the mayor of Dover. Photo courtesy National Archives

Meeting American servicemen and women was one of the high-lights of travel for ER, who, with her own sons in the military, had a motherly affection for these young people. ABOVE: The first lady signs an autograph for aviation radioman W. B. Allen, Pattern-maker First Class. C. J. Saunders looks on. U.S. Naval Air Station, San Juan, Puerto Rico. Photo U.S. Navy, courtesy National Archives

BELOW: Eleanor Roosevelt addresses apprentices at Boeing Airplane Company plant no. 2 in Seattle, Washington. The first lady is standing in front of the air-craft known as the "Flying Fortress," one of the most celebrated American war-planes during World War II. Her visit to Seattle was in support of the enormous defense production effort initiated by her husband in response to the demands of the war. Photo courtesy National Archives

ABOVE: ER eats with Marines at an air base at St. Thomas Virgin Islands during her Caribbean tour. Her secretary, Malvina Thompson, who accompanied her on several of her overseas trips and was her constant companion for decades, is in the back-ground. Photo courtesy National Archives

Eleanor and Franklin Roosevelt had an unusual partnership, one that saw them more often apart than together, but one that also allowed ER the unique freedom to pursue her own interests and her full agenda of public service activities. The Roosevelts weathered personal difficulties to work together while in the White House during the trying times of the Great Depression and World War II. LEFT: ER, FDR, and their dog, Fala, relax at Hyde Park. Photo courtesy National Archives

RIGHT: The Roosevelt family at Christmas 1944 at the family home in Hyde Park, New York. Pictured are three of the Roosevelts' children and seven of their grandchildren. All four Roosevelt sons served in the armed forces during World War II; two spent Christmas 1944 overseas. Pictured from left to right are grandson Curtis Boettiger; son Lieutenant Franklin D. Roosevelt, Jr., U.S. Navy, his wife, and their sons, Christopher and Franklin D. III; President Roosevelt; daughter Anna Boettiger and her son John (kneeling) and her daughter, Eleanor; Mrs. John Roosevelt and her daughter, Ann Sturgis, and her son, Haven; ER; and son Lieutenant John Roosevelt of the U.S. Navy. Photo by New York Times photos

ER's relationship with her mother-in-law remained somewhat strained throughout her marriage to Franklin. The elder Mrs. Roosevelt believed a woman's place was at home supporting her husband; she was never able to understand ER's independence and activism. LEFT: Eleanor Roosevelt rides in an open car with FDR and Sara Delano Roosevelt. Photo courtesy National Archives

ELEANOR ROOSEVELT, PRIVATE CITIZEN

BY JOSEPHINE RIPLEY

After her husband's death, Eleanor Roosevelt told journalists that "the story is over," but she found herself unable to retire from public life. Assessing her future after FDR's death, ER ruled out running for office in her own right and decided to focus on what she believed was her husband's greatest legacy, the United Nations. *LEFT:* ER walks onto the USS Franklin Delano Roosevelt at the New York Navy Yard in Brooklyn, New York, as part of the April 1945 launching ceremony for the 45,000-ton vessel named in honor of her late husband. Photo U.S. Navy, courtesy National Archives

After twelve years as the wife of the President of the United States, Eleanor Roosevelt closes the door of the White House behind her this week to become a private citizen.

No president's wife in the history of the country has traveled as widely or been as active in public affairs as Mrs. Roosevelt.

While the change which has come upon her so suddenly will lead her into different paths, few believe that it will mean her retirement from public life.

Eleanor Roosevelt has always been an active woman, keenly interested in people and in affairs. Since coming to the White House her viewpoint has broadened. She is a person who thinks today in terms of nations—the United Nations in which her husband had such hope.

She is not one of the great women thinkers of the day, but she is, nevertheless, a person of many talents and wide experience in various fields.

In her many speeches over the radio, she has required an admirable technique, a field in which the feminine voice meets its severest test.

"ALTHOUGH SOME HAVE CRITICIZED MRS. ROOSEVELT IN THE PAST FOR TAKING THE PROMINENT PART THAT SHE HAS IN PUBLIC AFFAIRS, THERE IS NOTHING BUT DEEP ADMIRATION TODAY FOR THE REMARKABLE FORTITUDE WITH WHICH SHE HAS MET THIS GREAT CRISIS IN HER LIFE."

She is equally at home on the lecture platform. She is the author of a number of books, including *The Moral Basis of Democracy, It's Up to the Women, This Is My Story,* and *My Days.*

Mrs. Roosevelt has written numerous magazine articles, and contributed the now famous "My Day" newspaper column.

Before coming to the White House, she edited a magazine called *Babies, Just Babies.* She was vice-principal of a school for girls. She founded and directed a furniture shop, and was actively interested in public housing as a member of the Housing Association of New York City.

She served at one time as State Democratic Committeewoman and has had a lifelong interest in social welfare. At the beginning of the war, Mrs. Roosevelt was made Assistant Director of the Office of Civilian Defense. Her administration of the job was severely criticized, however, and she resigned later.

Numerous avenues of activity which were closed to the wife of the President will undoubtedly open up to Eleanor Roosevelt, private citizen. There is no question but what the demand for her services will be many when she is ready to re-enter public life.

She would be the last to shirk what she feels to be her responsibility, and she has often stressed the responsibility of all citizens to do their part in helping to win the war and maintain the peace.

Last November, after the election, she told reporters that she thought the next four years would "probably be the most difficult the world has ever known, for we have to win a war, make a peace, and rebuild a world. I can't think of anything more difficult," she said.

After the Dumbarton Oaks Conference, she expressed the belief that "there should be a woman on every working committee." Not that women should take a dominant part in the peace-keeping, she explained, but that it is desirable for men and women to work together in that cause.

While the Nation, almost as stunned as Mrs. Roosevelt with the sudden change in her affairs, wonders what her role will be in the future, she herself is wholly occupied in moving out of the White House.

Upon her shoulders rests the responsibility of disposing of the 12-year accumulation of family belongings and the personal possessions of President Roosevelt, including his stamp collection, his marine prints, his ship models, and books.

But even with the burden of this task, she did not forget the new White House mistress would need help, and she spent more than an hour on Monday showing Mrs. Truman over the White House and explaining the duties which would be hers as First Lady of the Land.

Although some have criticized Mrs. Roosevelt in the past for taking the prominent part that she has in public affairs, there is nothing but deep admiration today for the remarkable fortitude with which she has met this great crisis in her life.

And the good wishes of millions all over the world follow her as she prepares to take up her new life as Eleanor Roosevelt, Citizen.

MY DAY: MAY 7, 1945

BY ELEANOR ROOSEVELT

President Franklin Delano Roosevelt died on April 12, 1945, at the "Little White House" in Warm Springs, Georgia. ER, who was in Washington at the time of her husband's death, traveled to Warm Springs to accompany his body back to the White House by train. A special cradle was built to hold the president's casket so that it was visible to the hundreds of thousands who lined the route to pay their final respects to the fallen leader. The train arrived in Union Station in Washington for a service at the White House before continuing on to Hyde Park for the president's burial. RIGHT: The president's casket visible through the window of the train. Photo courtesy National Archives

A friend of mine has just sent me a prayer by John Oxenham, a British poet. It is a very beautiful prayer for older people who have spent their lives so greatly that they fear not being able to give their best in their remaining years on earth:

"Lord, when Thou see'st that my work is done, Let me not linger here With failing powers, A workless worker in a world of work; But with a word, Just bid me Home And I will come, Right gladly will I come, Yea—Right gladly will I come—"

I have always felt that one could have a certain sense of resignation when people die who have lived long and fruitful lives. My rebellion has always been over the deaths of young people; and that is why I think so many of us feel particularly frustrated by war, when youth so largely pays the price. It seems as though youth was so much needed to carry the burden of peace.

A friend of mine, however, not long ago said something to me which may be comforting to other women. In speaking of her young son, she remarked that what she wanted for him was that he should feel that he had fulfilled his mission in life; that if he had not spent himself during this war fighting for the things in which he believed, he would feel empty. If he died and was [not] here to carry on in peacetime, she would still not rebel. She would know that to have denied him participation in the great adventure of fighting against the forces of evil, so that the forces of good might have an opportunity in the future to grow, would have left him warped and unable to carry on the battle for a better world in peace.

Of one thing I am sure: Young and old, in order to be useful we must stand for the things we feel are right, and we must work for those things wherever we find ourselves. It does very little good to believe something unless you tell your friends and associates of your beliefs. Those who fight down in the marketplace are bound to be confused now and then. Sometimes they will be deceived, and sometimes the dirt they touch will cling to them. But if their hearts are pure and their purposes unswerving, they will win through to the end of their mission on earth, untarnished.

From *My Day Volume II: The Post-War Years, Her Acclaimed Columns 1945–1952* by Eleanor Roosevelt. Reprinted by permission of United Feature Syndicate, Inc.

MY DAY: MAY 9, 1945; AUGUST 8, 1945

BY ELEANOR ROOSEVELT

"I cannot feel a spirit of celebration today," Eleanor Roosevelt wrote after the German surrender signaled the end of World War II in Europe. Mindful of the continued war in the Pacific, and of her own sons and the children of thousands of American families still in danger, she called for a renewed dedication to the cause of world peace. RIGHT: An Italian-American neighborhood in New York City celebrates the end of the war. Photo courtesy National Archives

MAY 9, 1945

All day yesterday, as I went about New York City, the words "V-E Day" were on everybody's lips. Part of the time, paper fluttered through the air until the gutter of the streets were filled with it. At Times Square crowds gathered—but that first report the other night had taken the edge off this celebration. No word came through from Washington and everybody still waited for official confirmation. Today it has come.

Over the radio this morning President Truman, Prime Minister Churchill and Marshal Stalin have all spoken—the war in Europe is over. Unconditional surrender has been accepted by the Germans. I can almost hear my husband's voice make that announcement, for I hear him repeat it so often. The German leaders were not willing to accept defeat, even when they knew it was inevitable, until they had made their people drink the last dregs in the cup of complete conquest by the Allies.

Europe is in ruins and the weary work of reconstruction must now begin. There must be joy, of course, in the hearts of the peoples whom the Nazis conquered and who are now free again. Freedom without bread, however, has little meaning. My husband always said that freedom from want and freedom from aggression were twin freedoms which had to go hand in hand.

The necessity to share with our brothers, even though it means hardship for ourselves, will now face all of us who live in the fortunate countries which war has not devastated.

I cannot feel a spirit of celebration today. I am glad that our men are no longer going to be shot at and killed in Europe, but the war in the Pacific still goes on. Men are dying there, even as I write. It is far more a day of dedication for us, a day on which to promise that we will do our utmost to end war and build peace. Some of my own sons, with millions of others, are still in danger.

I can but pray that the Japanese leaders will not force their people to complete destruction too. The ultimate end is sure, but in the hands of the Japanese leaders lies the decision of how many people will have to suffer before ultimate peace comes.

What are our ultimate objectives now? Do we want our Allies in Europe, and later in the Far East, to have the opportunity to rebuild quickly? Looked at selfishly, we will probably gain materially if they do. That cannot be our only responsibility, however. The men who fought this war are entitled to a chance to build a lasting peace. What we do in the next months may give them that chance or lose it for them. If we give people bread, we may build friendship among the peoples of the world; and we will never have peace without friendship around the world. This is the time for a long look ahead. This is the time for us all to decide where we go from here.

From *My Day Volume II: The Post-War Years, Her Acclaimed Columns 1945–1952* by Eleanor Roosevelt. Reprinted by permission of United Feature Syndicate, Inc.

AUGUST 8, 1945

The news which came to us yesterday afternoon of the first use of the atomic bomb in the war with Japan may have surprised a good many people, but scientists—both British and American—have been working feverishly to make this discovery before our enemies, the Germans, could make it and thereby possibly win the war.

This discovery may be of great commercial value someday. If wisely used, it may serve the purposes of peace. But for the moment we are chiefly concerned with its destructive power. That power can be multiplied indefinitely, so that not only whole cities but large areas may be destroyed at one fell swoop. If you face this possibility and realize that, having once discovered a principle, it is very easy to take steps to magnify its power, you soon face the unpleasant fact that in the next war whole peoples may be destroyed.

The only safe counter weapon to this new power is the firm decision of mankind that it shall be used for constructive purposes only. This discovery must spell the end of war. We have been paying an ever increasing price for indulging ourselves in this uncivilized way of settling our difficulties. We can no longer indulge in the slaughter of our young men. The price will be too high and will be paid not just by young men, but by whole populations.

In the past we have given lip service to the desire for peace. Now we meet the test of really working to achieve something basically new in the world. Religious groups have been telling us for a long time that peace could be achieved only by a basic change in the nature of man. I am inclined to think that this is true. But if we give human beings sufficient incentive, they may find good reason for reshaping their characteristics.

Good will among men was preached by the angels as they announced to the world the birth of the child Jesus. He exemplified it in His life and preached it Himself and sent forth His disciples, who have spread that gospel of love and human understanding throughout the world ever since. Yet the minds and hearts of men seemed closed.

Now, however, an absolute need exists for facing a nonescapable situation. This new discovery cannot be ignored. We have only two alternative choices: destruction and death—or construction and life! If we desire our civilization to survive, then we must accept the responsibility of constructive work and of the wise use of a knowledge greater than any ever achieved by man before.

From *My Day Volume II: The Post-War Years, Her Acclaimed Columns 1945–1952* by Eleanor Roosevelt. Reprinted by permission of United Feature Syndicate, Inc.

My Day: Undated, 1945; January 5, 1946

BY ELEANOR ROOSEVELT

UNDATED, 1945

When word was flashed that peace had come to the world again, I found myself filled with very curious sensations. I had no desire to go out and celebrate. I remembered the way that people demonstrated when the last war ended, but I felt this time that the weight of the suffering which has engulfed the world during so many years could not so quickly be wiped out. There is a quiet rejoicing that men are no longer bringing death to each other throughout the world. There is great happiness, too, in the knowledge that some day, soon, many of those we love will be at home again to give all they have to the rebuilding of a peaceful world.

One cannot forget, however, the many, many people to whom this day will bring only a keener sense of loss, for, as others come home, their loved ones will not return.

In every community, if we have eyes to see and hearts to feel, we will for many years see evidences of the period of war which we have been through. There will be men among us who all their lives, both physically and mentally, will carry the marks of war; and there will be women who mourn all the days of their lives. Yet there must be an undercurrent of deep joy in every human heart, and great thankfulness that we have world peace again.

The first days of peace require great statesmanship in our leaders. They are not easy days, for now we face the full results of the costs of war and must set ourselves to find the ways of building a peaceful world. The new atomic discovery has changed the whole aspect of the world in which we live. It has been primarily thought of in the light of its destructive power. Now we have to think of it in terms of how it may serve mankind in the days of peace.

This great discovery was not found by men of any one race or any one religion and its development and control should be under international auspices. All the world has a right to share in the beneficence which may grow from its proper development.

Great Britain and Canada and ourselves hold the secret today—and quite rightly, for we used its destructive force to bring the war to an end. But if we allow ourselves to think that any nation or any group of commercial interests should profit by something so great, we will eventually be the sufferers. God has shown great confidence in mankind when He allowed them wisdom and intelligence to discover this new secret. It is a challenge to us—the peoples who control the discovery—for unless we develop spiritual greatness commensurate with this new gift, we may bring economic war into the world and chaos instead of peace.

The greatest opportunity the world has ever had lies before us. God grant we have enough understanding of the divine love to live in the future as "one world" and "one people."

From *My Day Volume II: The Post-War Years, Her Acclaimed Columns 1945–1952* by Eleanor Roosevelt. Reprinted by permission of United Feature Syndicate, Inc.

JANUARY 5, 1946

have been thinking of the grave responsibility which lies not only on the delegates to the United Nations Organization but in the nation as a whole as we gather for our first meeting of the UNO Assembly.

On the success or failure of the United Nations Organization depend the preservation and continuance of our civilization.

We have learned how to destroy ourselves. Mankind can be wiped off the face of the earth by the action of any comparatively small group of people. So it would seem that if we care to survive we must progress in our social and economic development far more rapidly than we have done in the past.

We must, of course, lay proper stress in building this organization on the united force which will control all individual force throughout the world. At the same time, our real hope for the future lies in the development of a united economic, cultural, and social pattern.

This must increase the well-being of the peoples of the world. Otherwise, it will not win their loyalty and their constant, active participation and work as citizens. This is the only way in which we can hope to create the leadership needed in this organization to bring about the changes which can keep the world at peace.

The greed, suspicion and fear which have created wars in the past will create them again unless, through education and understanding, human beings can be brought to see that their own best interests lie along new lines of development. If we hope to prosper, others must prosper too, and if we hope to be trusted, we must trust others.

Above all, we must remember some of our ancient teachings which told us that a man could not guarantee the degree of development any other man might attain; but if he rose to his own greatest heights, willy-nilly, those around him would strive to achieve more than they would have without a great challenge.

The building of this organization is the greatest challenge that civilized man has ever faced. From earliest days he has fought for self-preservation, but always through destruction. Now, for the first time, he has reached a point where destruction can be so complete that he must find new ways to fight for self-preservation.

The building of a United Nations Organization is the way that lies before us today. Nothing else except security for all the peoples of the world will bring freedom from fear of destruction.

Security requires both control of the use of force and the elimination of want. No people are secure unless they have the things needed not only to preserve existence, but to make life worth living. These needs may differ widely now. They may change for all, from time to time. But all peoples throughout the world must know that there is an organization where their interests can be considered and where justice and security will be sought for all.

From *My Day Volume II: The Post-War Years, Her Acclaimed Columns 1945–1952* by Eleanor Roosevelt. Reprinted by permission of United Feature Syndicate, Inc.

Eleanor Roosevelt reacted to the news that World War II was ended with what she called "curious sensations." The news of peace brought relief and great joy; yet at the same time, having seen the suffering and devastation of the war firsthand in her travels, she understood that for many the scars of war would not quickly fade. In her daily newspaper column, "My Day," the former first lady urged Americans to temper their celebrations of the war's end with serious reflection on the meaning of war and of peace and on their responsibilities not just as Americans but as citizens of the world. LEFT: ER shares lunch with the enlisted men at the Natal, Philippines, air base. Photo courtesy National Archives

Eleanor Roosevelt (signature)

WITH THE UNITED NATIONS IN LONDON

BY ELEANOR ROOSEVELT

Eleanor Roosevelt brought to her work at the United Nations, "a real good will for people throughout the world." She lobbied hard for the rights of poor working families, women in the workplace, minorities in the armed forces, and children in every walk of life. UN organizers recognized ER's passion for humanitarianism and appointed her to the committee charged with drafting a universal declaration on human rights. The resolution was adopted in 1948. Cynics doubted the value of the declaration, but ER believed that it was a beginning. "Where, after all," she remarked, "do human rights begin? In small places, close to home. . . . Such are the places where every man, woman and child seeks equal justice, equal opportunity, equal dignity without discrimination. Unless these rights have meaning there, they have little meaning anywhere." ABOVE: ER displays a copy of the Universal Declaration of Human Rights. Photo United Nations, courtesy National Archives

Now I want to turn back to late in 1945 when there began one of the wonderful and, I hope, worthwhile experiences in my life. At that time I still had my apartment on Washington Square at the lower end of Fifth Avenue. . . .

While I was living there in December of 1945 I received a message from President Truman. He reminded me that the first or organizing meeting of the United Nations General Assembly would be held in London, starting in January 1946, and he asked me if I would serve as a member of the United States delegation.

"Oh, no! It would be impossible," was my first reaction. "How could I be a delegate to help organize the United Nations when I have no background or experience in international meetings?"

Miss Thompson, however, urged me not to decline without giving the idea careful thought. I knew in a general way what had been done about organizing the United Nations. After the San Francisco meeting in 1945 when the Charter was written it had been accepted by the various nations, including our own, through their constitutional processes. I knew, too, that we had a group of people headed by Adlai Stevenson working with representatives of other member nations in London to prepare for the formal organizing meeting. Then, as I thought about the President's offer, I knew that I believed the United Nations to be the one hope for a peaceful world. I knew that my husband had placed great importance on the establishment of this world organization. So I felt a great sense of responsibility.

I talked it over with Tommy and with my son Elliot, and with various other friends, all of whom urged me to accept. At last, I did so in fear and trembling. But I might not have done it if I had not known at that time that President Truman could only nominate me as a delegate and that the nomination would have to be approved by the United States Senate, where certain Senators would disapprove of me because of my attitude toward social problems and more especially youth problems. . . . Anyway, my nomination was confirmed by the Senate, and I still marvel at it.

There was not much time left before the delegates were to leave for London and I had to get ready in a hurry after receiving all kinds of instructions from the Department of State. . . .

I did not know that I was permitted to take a secretary with me to the meeting in London—one had to be assigned to me later—and when I said good-by to Tommy I was rather heavy hearted at the thought of crossing the Atlantic Ocean alone in January. I had always been a bad sailor, although somehow in the years that my husband had been Assistant Secretary of the Navy I had learned not to be seasick. Members of the delegation sailed on the *Queen Elizabeth* and the

dock was swarming with reporters and news photographers who surrounded the Senators and Congressmen on the delegation to get last-minute statements and pictures. Everything had quieted down, however, when I drove in my own car to the dock and got aboard rather late and managed to find my way to my stateroom. . . .

People on the *Queen Elizabeth* were very kind to me, but nevertheless I felt much alone at first. One day, as I was walking down the passageway to my cabin, I encountered Senator Arthur H. Vandenberg, a Republican and before the war a great champion of isolationism. He stopped me.

"Mrs. Roosevelt," he said in his rather deep voice, "we would like to know if you would serve on Committee 3."

I had two immediate and rather contradictory reactions to the question. First, I wondered who "we" might be. Was a Republican Senator deciding who would serve where? And why, since I was a delegate, had I not been consulted about committee assignments? But my next reaction crowded these thoughts out of my mind. I suddenly realized that I had no more idea than the man in the moon what Committee 3 might be. So I kept my thoughts to myself and humbly agreed to serve where I was asked to serve. . . .

After our ship docked at Southampton and we were all officially greeted, I drove to London with Senator and Mrs. Tom Connally. I had once spent three years at school in England at Allenswood so I knew what the English villages and country estates looked like before the war. But now there were signs everywhere of what the war years had done. Broken fences might have been expected at home, perhaps, but until now I had never seen any on an English estate. Trees were down and the woods uncared for. Driving through villages, we saw gaps between houses with new, low brick walls in front of what had been a house. To American eyes this kind of thing looked natural enough even after we were in the suburbs of London. Senator Connally remarked that the war damage did not seem great. So I pointed out where the still-standing front of a house often hid complete destruction behind or where there was a neat fence around a hole where a building had once stood. In America we are always tearing down and building up. In England everything remains the same for hundreds of years and I realized that somehow we Americans would have to try to see with British eyes if we were to understand what these scenes meant to them.

As I learned more about my work I realized why I had been put on Committee 3, which dealt with humanitarian, educational, and cultural questions. There were many committees dealing with the budgetary, legal, political and other questions, and I could just see the gentlemen of our delegation puzzling over the list and saying: "Oh, no! We can't put

Mrs. Roosevelt on the political committee. What could she do on the budget committee? Does she know anything about legal questions? Ah, here's the safe spot for her—Committee 3. She can't do much harm there!"

Oddly enough, I felt very much the same way about it. On the ship coming over, however, State Department officials had held "briefings" for the delegates. We listened to experts on various subjects explain the problems that would be brought up, give the background on them and then state the general position of the United States on various controversial points. I attended all these sessions and, discovering there also were briefings for newspaper people aboard the ship, I went to all their meetings, too. As a result of these briefings and of my talks with Mr. [Durward] Sandifer and others, I began to realize that Committee 3 might be much more important than had been expected. And, in time, this proved to be true. . . .

At the early sessions in London, which were largely concerned with technicalities of organization, I got the strong impression that many of the old-timers in the field of diplomacy were very skeptical of the new world organization. They had seen so many failures, they had been through the collapse of the League of Nations, and they seemed to doubt that we would achieve much. The newcomers, the younger people in most cases, were the ones who showed the most enthusiasm and determination; they were, in fact, often almost too anxious to make progress.

I might point out here that during the entire London session of the Assembly I walked on eggs. I knew that as the only woman on the delegation I was not very welcome. Moreover, if I failed to be a useful member, it would not be considered merely that I as an individual had failed, but that all women had failed, and there would be little chance for others to serve in the near future.

I tried to think of small ways in which I might be more helpful. There were not too many women on the other delegations, and as soon as I got to know some of them I invited them all to tea in my sitting room at the hotel. About sixteen, most of them alternate delegates or advisers, accepted my invitation. Even the Russian woman came, bringing an interpreter with her. The talk was partly just social but as we became better acquainted we also talked about the problems on which we were working on the various committees. The party was so successful that I asked them again on other occasions, either as a group or a few at a time. I discovered that in such informal sessions we sometimes made more progress in reaching an understanding on some question before the United Nations than we had been able to achieve in the formal work of our committees. . . .

As a normal thing, the important—and, I might say, the hard—work of any organization such as the United Nations is not done in the big, public meetings of the General Assembly, but in the small and almost continuous meetings of the various committees. In the committee meetings each nation is represented by one delegate or an alternate delegate and two or three advisers. Committees meet in smaller rooms and sit at desks arranged in a large circle. They elect officers and, if the chairman of the committee is a capable

Eleanor Roosevelt was at first reluctant when President Harry Truman nominated her as a delegate to the United Nations. She worried that without true experience in foreign relations she would be ineffective in the world body. But Truman was adamant, and on the urging of her family—and bolstered by her own belief that the United Nations was her husband's greatest legacy—she accepted the challenge and became one of the most active, effective voices the United Nations has ever known. RIGHT: ER speaks to the delegates at the United Nations. Photo United Nations, courtesy National Archives

taskmaster, a great deal of work can be done. A proposal of a plan or a project must be thoroughly talked over and, if possible, agreed upon by a committee before it is presented to the General Assembly for final debate and a vote.

So, the discussions and the compromises and the disagreements that occur in committee meetings are of the utmost importance. Personally, I always found such sessions more interesting than the plenary sessions of the Assembly. At first, of course, I was not familiar with committee work and not at all sure of myself, but Mr. Sandifer was always seated just behind me to give me guidance. As time went on I got so I could tell merely by his reactions whether the discussion was going well or badly. If I could feel him breathing down my neck I knew that there was

trouble coming, usually from the Russians. But at other times when I felt that our opponents in some debate were getting out of hand, he would remain quiet and calm. "Just sit tight," he would whisper. "It will be all right. With these fellows you have to be patient."

There is a question many persons have asked me about the responsibilities of a delegate to the United Nations: "You are representing your government," they say, "but do you do exactly what you are told to do or say? Do you have any latitude for self-expression or for personal judgment in voting?"

The answer is perhaps a little complicated. In the first committee meetings I attended, in London, I was in complete agreement with the position of the State Department on the question at issue: the right of war refugees to decide for themselves whether they would return to their countries of origin. I was a little uncertain about procedure, however, and often I lagged behind when the chairman called for a vote. Finally, Mr. Sandifer said sternly:

"The United States is an important country. It should vote quickly because certain other countries may be waiting to follow its leadership. So you must vote promptly."

After that, you may be sure that I always tried to decide just how I would vote before a show of hands was asked for and, as soon as it was, my hand went up with alacrity. In deciding how to vote, it is true that a delegate, as a representative of his government, is briefed in advance on his country's position in any controversy. At London, fortunately, I agreed with the State Department position, because I do not think I would have dared to question it. But later I learned that a delegate does have certain rights as an individual, and on several occasions I exercised my right to take a position somewhat different from the official viewpoint. . . .

However, it was while working on Committee 3 that I really began to understand the inner workings of the United Nations. It was ironical perhaps that one of the subjects that created the greatest political heat of the London sessions came up in this "unimportant" committee to which I had been assigned.

The issue, which I have already referred to, arose from the fact that there were many displaced war refugees in Germany when the armistice was signed . . . a great number of whom were still living there in temporary camps because they did not want to return to live under the Communist rule of their own countries. There also were the pitiful Jewish survivors of the German death camps.

I do not suppose that it had been generally foreseen that this situation would lead to a headline controversy in London, but it did and it flared up in Committee 3. It was raised originally by the Yugoslav representative, Leo

Mates, a quick, bright young man whom I came to know well and who became Ambassador to Washington. Mr. Mates was engagingly innocent-looking and we often exchanged sympathetic smiles when we were both bored by some long-winded speaker. But he was highly skilled in his job, he knew how to take advantage of every parliamentary trick and, if he fooled you into letting down your guard for one instant, he would win his point every time. I learned to watch him with care. In later years I acquired a great respect for his ability and as he grew older and after his country had been broken with Soviet Cominform we began to see some things from more nearly the same point of view. But at that first meeting of Committee 3 he was my very dangerous adversary.

The Yugoslav—and, of course, the Soviet Union—position that Mates put forward was that any war refugee who did not wish to return to his country of origin was either a quisling or a traitor to his country. He argued that the refugees in Germany should be forced to return home and to accept whatever punishment might be meted out to them. This position was strongly supported by the Soviet representative, Professor Amazap A. Arutiunian, an Armenian who ably served for a long time in the Russian delegation.

The position of the Western countries, including the United States, was that large numbers of the refugees were neither quislings nor traitors and that they must be guaranteed the right to choose whether or not they would return to their homes. Since the London sessions were largely technical rather than political debates and since Committee 3 was the scene of one of the early clashes between the Soviet Union and the West, the newspapers found it convenient to make much of the refugee controversy. I felt very strongly on the subject, as did others, and we spent countless hours trying to frame some kind of resolution on which all could agree. We never did, and our chairman, Peter Fraser of New Zealand, had to present a majority report to the General Assembly which was immediately challenged by the USSR.

In the Assembly the minority position was handled, not by the Soviet representative on Committee 3, but by the head of the Soviet Union's delegation, Andrei Vishinsky. It might be mentioned here that most nations would have had their committee representative discuss the question before the Assembly, since he presumably would be more familiar with the subject. But the Russians had a highly effective way of making the head of their delegation responsible for every subject that came up in the Assembly.

Vishinsky was one of the Russians' great legal minds, a skilled debater, a man with ability to use the weapons of wit and ridicule. And Moscow apparently considered the refugee question of such vital importance that he spoke before the Assembly in a determined effort to win over the delegates to the Communist point of view. The British representative on our committee spoke in favor of the majority report. By this time an odd situation had developed. It was apparent that in view of the importance of the issue someone would have to speak for the United States. The question of who this was to be threw our delegation into a veritable dither. There was a hurried and rather uncomfortable consultation among the male members and when the huddle broke up John Foster Dulles approached me rather uncertainly.

"Mrs. Roosevelt," he began, rather lamely, "the United States must speak in the debate. Since you are the one who has carried on for us in this controversy in the committee, do you think you could say a few words to the Assembly? I'm afraid nobody else is really familiar with the subject."

"Why, Mr. Dulles," I replied as meekly as I could manage, "in that case I will do my best." . . .

I trembled at the thought of speaking against the famous Mr. Vishinsky. But when the time came I walked, tense and excited, to the rostrum and did my best. There was a little more than met the eye in this situation. The hour was late and we knew the Russians would delay a vote as long as possible on the theory that some of our allies would get tired and leave. I knew we must, if possible, hold our South American colleagues until the vote was taken because their votes might be decisive. So I talked about Simon Bolivar and his stand for the freedom of the People of Latin America. I talked and watched the delegates and to my joy the South American representatives stayed with us to the end and, when the vote came, we won.

This vote meant that the Western nations would have to worry about the ultimate fate of the refugees for a long, long time, but the principle of the right of an individual to make his own decisions was a victory well worth while. . . .

As the London sessions neared their end the austerity of life in Great Britain may have become more burdensome to us, although we suffered very few of the hardships that the British endured in their homes. Among other things, however, it was almost impossible to get eggs even at Claridge's hotel. For this reason, I was particularly touched one day when a lady who lived on a farm came to London and brought me half a dozen eggs.

That same morning Congressman Sol Bloom distressed me by saying that he was going home. Mr. Bloom was an expert on parliamentary procedure and served on the committee on rules. On one occasion I had complained to him that his committee seemed to talk endlessly; that

they haggled for hours whether to use this word or that word in a resolution. I asked if the rules must be so precisely worded. Mr. Bloom severely reprimanded me.

"These things," he said, "are more important than you know. When you are working in a parliamentary body you understand eventually the importance of using the right word in the right place. The phrasing of a sentence or the use of a word may later be of great importance in enabling you to win a particular point in a debate. Or it may cause you to lose a point."

I never forgot the lesson he taught me and tried to overcome my impatience, and because I greatly enjoyed knowing him, his decision to go home before the session ended caused me to protest.

"No," he replied, "I am going home tomorrow. In my entire life I have never been without two eggs for breakfast each morning. Here I find it impossible to get anything but those horrible powdered eggs. I am going home."

At this point I had an inspiration. I promptly handed him the half dozen eggs that had just been presented to me. "Now," I said, "will you please stay at least three more days?"

"Yes," he said. "I will stay."

By the end of the three days, Senator Francis Townsend of Maryland, who was an alternate on our delegation, had discovered that he could have eggs flown over from Canada. So we were able to keep the valuable services of Congressman Bloom through the rest of the session.

Toward the end of the sessions we worked until late at night. The final night the vote on Committee 3's report was taken so late that I did not get back to the hotel till about one o'clock. I was very tired, and as I walked wearily up the stairs at the hotel I heard two voices behind me. Turning around, I saw Senator Vandenberg and Mr. Dulles. They obviously had something to say to me, but for the life of me I can't recall which one of them said it. Whichever it was, he seemed to be speaking for both.

"Mrs. Roosevelt," he said, "we must tell you that we did all we could to keep you off the United States delegation. We begged the President not to nominate you. But now that you are leaving we feel we must acknowledge that we have worked with you gladly and found you good to work with. And we will be happy to do so again."

I don't think anything could have made the weariness drop from my shoulders as did those words. I shall always be grateful for the encouragement they gave me.

NUMBER ONE
WORLD CITIZEN

BY RALPH G. MARTIN

Because polio had affected her own life so dramatically, Eleanor Roosevelt was very aware of the devastation that the disease could bring to its victims; and she was active in fundraising for polio research. ABOVE: ER is shown with her successor as first lady, Bess Truman, along with fourteen-year-old film actress Peggy Ann Garner, during a radio broadcast opening "motion picture collection week" for the March of Dimes, the charity begun by FDR to raise money to combat polio. Photo by New York Times Photos

It was a beautiful exhibition of diplomatic fencing, but there wasn't much of an audience to appreciate it. At this meeting of the UN Human Rights Commission, the French and Russian delegates were both getting overwhelmed when Mrs. Roosevelt broke in. Hers was the patient voice of common sense and when she had finished, the sharp edges of the discussion had been smoothed.

Talking about it afterwards, Mrs. Roosevelt's pretty blond assistant, Mrs. Trude Lash, shook her head in amazement.

"We've been trying to get Mrs. Roosevelt to stay in bed this week, but she wouldn't do it. You know what she has? She has shingles, and it's so terribly painful that I don't see how she can sit still, much less conduct a meeting intelligently. But she hasn't missed a session. Because she knows how important it is to get this thing started right. That woman isn't just the wife of a great President, she is the great wife of a great President."

Sitting in her small, homey New York office, Mrs.Roosevelt's eyes were gently serious and she looked straight at you when she spoke: "I'm ashamed," she said, "I'm really ashamed because we've made so few plans for our returning veterans. It seems that the majority of the American people prefer to wait until things fall on their heads before they do anything. We should have started preparing for peace a long time ago. . . ."

She hesitated for a minute, staring at the bust of her husband on the nearby desk, then went on. "Everybody blames Congress for not doing the planning and Congress deserves a big share of the blame, but it's the people themselves who are mostly at fault. If the people had put the pressure on Congress, if they had constantly made known their wishes, there might be more housing, more jobs, more of everything today.

"It's a very good thing to allow veterans to go to college, but look how many veterans are finding colleges too crowded to take them in. Also, it's a fine thing to offer veterans loans to buy homes, but there are no homes to buy. As for jobs, a few towns did some intelligent planning, but darn few!

"It just isn't fair. . . ."

One of the museum curators up at Hyde Park was discussing FDR's "magic touch" in always knowing the changing mood of the American people.

"Only there was nothing magic about it," he said. "If you ask me, it was Eleanor Roosevelt. The way she traveled all over the country, talking and listening to all kinds of people. And the huge piles of daily mail that she read so carefully. It was Eleanor who came to him and gave him the pulse of the people."

Sitting inside the air-cooled restaurant, the tall, kindly looking lawyer reminisced about the times he had visited the White House and the Roosevelts.

"In my opinion," he stated, "he had the deepest respect for her judgment. He had so many yes-men around him that he needed a few people to say no sometimes, and she was one of the few. What's more, she would always fight for what she believed in. And when they disagreed, he knew he couldn't kid her out of anything. Sure, she was his Minister without Portfolio on Social Conditions, but in many ways she was also his conscience. . . ."

In the quiet library at the Women's Trade Union League, where Eleanor Roosevelt once taught a class in literature, the small, thin president spoke:

"I remember that party we gave for her before she left for the White House in 1932. Somebody wrote a song kidding her about how she would have to be so careful of everything she said and did and tone down her social conscience and have a lot of pink tea parties.

"And I'll never forget what she said when the song was over. The way she stood up and smiled and said, so firmly, 'I shall be myself, as always.'"

Mrs. Roosevelt leaned back just a little, her head almost under the sketch of her husband. "One thing does make me happy," she said. "The fact that many veterans seem more world-conscious, more serious-minded than they ever were.

"Take my Frankie, for example," she said softly. "He was just a young, lovable kid. Now he's so much more serious about things, he's so much more willing to work for what he believes in. The American Veterans Committee, for example."

She thought the AVC was a good idea because she felt the younger men of this war needed their own organization. Although she thought that liberal veterans should join the older organizations to make their pressure felt, her opinion was that ultimately they would switch to their own World War II outfit.

"The trouble with the older organizations," she continued, "is that the older men try to swamp the younger veterans with stories of what they did on the last war. We all do that when we get older. I often catch myself doing it, even though I try hard not to."

But, besides that, she liked the AVC idea of "citizens first, veterans second." Because if the veterans set themselves aside as a special class and push for super-seniority in such things as civil service, then they can not only ruin civil service but they can ruin the whole country. . . ."

Graying Malvina Thompson shook her head. "I've been her secretary for so many years and I still don't know how she does it. Always on the move somewhere. Always a speech to make or an important meeting to go to or some people to see. This morning alone I turned down 43 invitations."

Then there were the hundreds of camps she had visited overseas, always insisting that there be no dress parades. She knew that the soldiers hated to wait for hours just so somebody could look at them for a few minutes.

"And we must have walked through miles and miles of hospitals," Miss Thompson added.

There was that one in England where, as usual, Mrs. Roosevelt insisted on stopping at every bed in every ward. Puffing along behind her was a fat colonel who finally interrupted, "Mrs. Roosevelt, we have spent much more time here than we were supposed to. We're supposed to meet the general and the lord mayor for lunch and we're late already."

Mrs. Roosevelt simply smiled and said, "There's only one more ward, Colonel. . . ."

The young man in the Hungarian restaurant was saying that Mrs. Roosevelt was probably the worst hated and the best-loved woman in the world. All those vicious attacks by the Peglers and the O'Donnells and the Southern reactionaries, and the twisted cranks who wrote her during the war, "I hope all your sons get killed"—those things didn't bother her deeply, except when they struck at her through her close friends.

And whenever she addressed any meetings there were always one or two people who popped up with malicious questions.

"I'll never forget the woman who asked her in a loud voice, 'Mrs. Roosevelt, isn't it true that the President's illness affected his mind?'

"There was a long pause and then she answered, slowly, 'Yes, I think it did. I think it made him more sensitive to the feelings of suffering people. . . .'"

"What I can't understand," said Mrs. Roosevelt, "is why so many newspapers and magazines and even the general public have been attacking the United Nations instead of boosting it. Doesn't everybody know by now that the United Nations is our last big hope for peace in this world?"

As for crises, of course there are going to be crises, she said. But they shouldn't be over-exaggerated. "I never once heard Franklin admit that there was any crisis that couldn't be peaceably solved."

Her voice was quieter when she said, "It's up to the veterans to keep this nation welded together. It's up to them to be the loudest, strongest pressure group for the United Nations and peace. If not, we might not have a world. . . ."

The American UN delegates had just come back from their tour of the DP [Displaced Persons] camps in Europe and Mrs. Roosevelt asked them what they had seen.

Oh, it wasn't so bad, they said, those DP camps weren't really so bad as they were painted. They had talked to a lot of army officers about it and they had gone on a conducted tour of some of the camps.

"But did you talk to the DPs?" she wanted to know.

No they hadn't. It had never occurred to them.

Her voice was strained. "How can you know anything, unless you talk to the people themselves? . . ."

From *New Republic*, August 5, 1946.

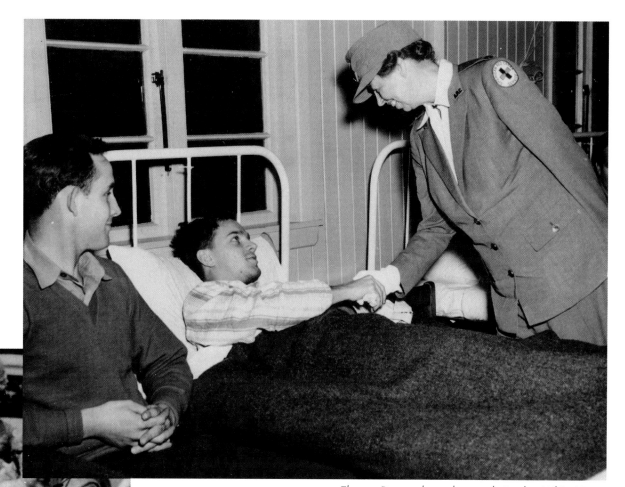

Eleanor Roosevelt was known during her White House years as "First Lady of the World"; and after her husband's death, her status in the eyes of the public did not change. Many Americans continued to think of ER as the first lady for the remainder of her life. ABOVE: ER visits Marines in a hospital in New Zealand. Photo U.S. Marine Corps, courtesy National Archives

LEFT: The first lady sits on the ground with soldiers on the lawn of the White House during a garden party for the unit of soldiers responsible for guarding the White House after the bombing of Pearl Harbor. Photo courtesy National Archives

Eleanor Roosevelt

My Day: May 6, 1947;
July 26, 1945

BY ELEANOR ROOSEVELT

Although FDR's will guaranteed ER and her children a life interest in the Roosevelt family home, Springwood, in Hyde Park, New York, ER turned the estate over to the United States government as a museum shortly after the president's death. She purchased the land surrounding Val-Kill, however, and made the cottage her permanent home for the remainder of her life. While at Val-Kill, ER began a daily ritual of walking the many acres with the president's Scottish Terrier, Fala. FDR's will had left the dog to a friend, thinking ER would not have the time to care for him; but her children asked that the dog be returned to their mother, and the two became devoted companions. LEFT: ER with Fala at Val-Kill in November of 1951. Photo courtesy Franklin D. Roosevelt Library

May 6, 1947

About a month ago, our farmer told us and proved to us that it was highly uneconomical to make butter on a dairy farm; that we could sell our whole milk and make more cash; that the cost of the cream and the time consumed in making butter, even though we had an electric churn, was pure waste.

I remembered that, when I was a little girl, my grandmother made butter in a little glass churn on the dining-room table. It was completely sweet fresh butter, and we thought it the greatest possible luxury. And my mother-in-law always boasted of having her own butter. It seemed somewhat of a wrench to me to give this up, so I loftily said to our farmer, "I will take the churn and in our cellar we will make enough butter to last both my son's house and mine for several weeks. It can be stored in the deep freeze."

Last Friday, the farmer brought the churn. Our superintendent was on hand. So was I, assisted by Miss Thompson and the cook. We all stood around, prepared for our first lesson.

The farmer first showed us how to wash the churn and the implements. Then, firmly telling me the cost of the cream which he was pouring in, he poured it in, adjusted the cover of the churn, and started it. All of us were spattered with cream. He stopped the churn, looked at the cork at the bottom, adjusted the top, and started the churn again.

Then the five of us watched with pride for fifteen minutes while the electricity did its work. Finally, I inquired how long it took. The farmer said, "Anywhere from twenty minutes to four hours. It depends on the temperature." I thought he meant the outdoor temperature and did not realize that he meant the temperature of the cream, which in our haste we had forgotten to take.

Time wore on. Miss Thompson decided she had to go back to being a secretary. The two men decided they had to go and eat dinner and attend to a few chores. The cook decided she had to go and prepare lunch. So we left the churning!

Three hours later, I returned. Still no butter. The men tried putting in ice cubes, which spoiled the buttermilk. It came time for the men to do that afternoon's chores and so they said, "Leave it overnight and turn it on in the morning and the butter may come."

The next morning, around 11 o'clock, the cook and I finally finished our lesson and at last the men could go back to their work on the farm. We had learned how to use the electric churn, how to work the butter afterwards, and how to do it neatly up in half-pound packages. For all of that time and all of that labor, we had 13½ pounds of butter!

I am quite sure now that our farmer's economics are correct, but I had fun and I think the cook and I will try it again. It may be a waste of both time and money, but I am still old-fashioned enough to like the idea of having my own butter. I am rather glad, however, that the churn is electric. I think if I had had to churn by hand for all that time, I would not be writing about it today.

From *My Day Volume II: The Post-War Years, Her Acclaimed Columns 1945–1952* by Eleanor Roosevelt. Reprinted by permission of United Feature Syndicate, Inc.

JULY 26, 1945

The rain has been wonderful for the woods. As I walk every morning with Fala, I realize that it is a long time since I have seen our little planted pines make such a growth, or found such luxuriance of foliage everywhere. It is a grand year for mosquitoes, too. Sometimes I think that I'll never walk past some of our swamps again till autumn, but then the beauty of their ferns draws me back.

Fala, too, has such a wonderful time hunting whatever may be the hidden things in that particular part of the woods that I can't bear not to take him there. Occasionally, he gets a scent and disappears entirely. I can't stand and wait for him, because the mosquitoes then settle on me with too much ease. So I walk on just as fast as possible, meanwhile singing in unmusical fashion and as loudly as possible all the hymns I can remember from my childhood days. That seems to bring Fala back more quickly than calling him by name.

Our garden has done pretty well and we are getting vegetables in great quantity, but my family has been so large all summer that I have not had a chance to put as much into the freezer as I otherwise might have done. In August, however, I shall have to be away from here for a time, and I am counting on putting many things up for the winter months. My freezer, which is a new acquisition, makes it possible to plan for the future and use one's surplus.

This is a quiet life we lead up here, but it seems nevertheless to be a busy one. People are coming to tea today, and late this afternoon Postmaster General and Mrs. Hannegan, Paul Fitzpatrick and Miss Doris Byrne, chairman and vice-chairman respectively of the Democratic State Committee, are all coming to spend the night. Tomorrow we attend the ceremonies at the post office when the stamp issued in memory of my husband, showing the Hyde Park house, is first put on sale.

From *My Day Volume II: The Post-War Years, Her Acclaimed Columns 1945–1952* by Eleanor Roosevelt. Reprinted by permission of United Feature Syndicate, Inc.

Eleanor Roosevelt (signature)

My Day: July 16, 1947;
July 26, 1947

by Eleanor Roosevelt

Eleanor Roosevelt had mixed feelings about the Roosevelt family vacation home at Campobello Island, New Brunswick, Canada. She first visited the island in 1904 during her courtship. After her marriage, she generally spent summers there with her growing family, as Franklin came and went depending upon his political schedule. In these years, ER often felt alone and isolated at Campobello. It was also at Campobello that Franklin was stricken with polio and where ER nursed him through the darkest days of his illness. Later in life, ER learned to cherish the beauty and peace of the island and also to recall the many happy family times spent there. After her husband's death, she continued to spend summer weeks at Campobello with her children, her grandchildren, and her close friends. ABOVE AND RIGHT: ER and her family at Campobello Island in the early 1920s. Photos courtesy Franklin D. Roosevelt Library

JULY 16, 1947

This morning we are off to Maine—eight adults, four children, three dogs, one a puppy only a few months old, two cars, and a truck loaded with bicycles, bags, typewriters, and books. This evening we are going to descend, we hope, on Ogunquit, Maine, to see my daughter-in-law, Faye Emerson Roosevelt, act in "State of the Union." Then we will proceed to Campobello Island, New Brunswick, to spend a month there in strict retirement—devoting half of each day to work on a book and the other half to all the things that our youngsters love to do in a place where life is lived largely upon the water.

One thing which draws me back to this remote island is the sunsets as I look from my porch across the water to the mainland, where two rivers flow in on either side of Eastport, Maine. The sun sets behind the little town.

Eastport and Lubec are the two nearest mainland towns. They are not so very picturesque when you are in the streets, but from across the water they have great charm. I have sometimes thought that Lubec might almost be Mont St. Michel on the coast of France. That is just a little stretch of the imagination, however, and I like both these little towns for what they are. I get a lift of the spirit as soon as I begin to breathe the sea air of the Maine coast.

"I GET A LIFT OF THE SPIRIT AS SOON AS I BEGIN TO BREATHE THE SEA AIR OF THE MAINE COAST."

From *My Day Volume II: The Post-War Years, Her Acclaimed Columns 1945–1952* by Eleanor Roosevelt. Reprinted by permission of United Feature Syndicate, Inc.

JULY 26, 1947

Fog, which lifts every day for only a short time, but always hangs just over the edge of the island, becomes pretty monotonous—and, until yesterday, that is the kind of weather we have had ever since we arrived here. Someone told me that the people out on Grand Manan Island have been enveloped in fog for 47 days, and I doubt if it has even lifted in the daytime. But a good many of that island's summer visitors are artists and some of the fog effects in this region can be very beautiful. Nevertheless, every one of us greeted with joy the sunshine and the clearing west wind yesterday.

We packed our lunch baskets and in my son's little power boat we started up the St. Croix River for St. Andrews. Some of our guests had an orgy of shopping at the craft shop there, since wool is again available and the hand-woven materials, blankets, and so on, are very well made and very attractive.

Finally, we went to the little island just across the harbor from the town of St. Andrews. We built a fire between two rocks, scrambled our eggs, cooked our bacon, and fed a hungry crowd.

It seemed the right spot to read Longfellow's "Evangeline" to the children, and so I told them the story of Nova Scotia and the Acadian peasants, and then read from a book that had belonged to their grandfather.

"This is the forest primeval. The murmuring pines and the hemlocks bearded with moss and in garments green, indistinct in the twilight, stand like druids of old. . . ."

Few people read Longfellow anymore and yet I think he is part of our heritage, both literary and historical. And any child who is not familiar with his poems misses something.

I have read a good deal more to the older children up here than to the younger ones. But the other night we found a copy of "Uncle Remus" which belonged to their father, and the little ones were enthralled. However, I found it difficult to read aloud. It really, I imagine, requires a true Southerner to do it justice.

With the older children I have read "The Jungle Book" and we are now deep in a book—which belonged to their Uncle James—called "Connie Morgan in Alaska." It is curious how some books can go on from generation to generation and still hold one's interest. So much that is written deals with contemporary thoughts and situations, but apparently a good story remains enjoyable. We have come across some copies of David Gray's "Gallops" and "Ensign Russell," and all of us, young and old, have enjoyed them.

From *My Day Volume II: The Post-War Years, Her Acclaimed Columns 1945–1952* by Eleanor Roosevelt. Reprinted by permission of United Feature Syndicate, Inc.

LIFE WITH ELEANOR

BY HAROLD LAVINE

In 1948, Eleanor Roosevelt at first refused to publicly support President Harry S. Truman in his bid for a second term in office. As the election drew nearer, however, ER, impressed by Truman's tough and no-nonsense campaigning, and also aware of the value of her support to the Democratic Party, offered her official endorsement. In a radio address from France, ER stated that "there has never been a campaign where a man has shown more personal courage and confidence in the people of the United States," and she threw her support behind Truman. RIGHT: President Truman and ER. Photo courtesy National Archives

Ordinarily the wives of Presidents retire into obscurity when their husbands leave the White House, and Presidents' widows disappear completely from the public view. Until a year ago [1948] there were four widows of former Presidents still living, but only a handful of Americans could name the other three. Mrs. Eleanor Roosevelt is still front-page news. Without disrespect to Mrs. Harry S. Truman, millions still think of the widow of FDR as First Lady of the United States. To millions more, she is First Lady of the world.

Every survey made has shown that she is the best known woman in the world, the best-loved, and the most influential. In its February 1948 issue the *Woman's Home Companion* . . . asked its readers: "Who is your favorite American?" Mrs. Roosevelt led all the rest, running ahead of General Dwight D. Eisenhower, former Secretary of State George C. Marshall, General Douglas MacArthur, and president Truman—in that order. Mrs. Roosevelt was then writing for the *Companion*'s rival, the *Ladies Home Journal*. Last December, the Gallup poll asked: "What woman anywhere in the world do you most admire?" Again Mrs. Roosevelt headed the list, followed by Mme. Chiang Kai-shek and Sister Kenny.

When she visited England last year to unveil a memorial to FDR and to receive an honorary degree from Oxford, *The London Daily Herald* declared: "She is . . . a big and generous personality, a worker for all just causes, a woman who would have won fame had she never married a famous man."

However, the admiration of Mrs. Roosevelt is by no means unanimous. She has been severely criticized for failing to comply with the notion that woman's place is in the home. The long record of divorce among her children, a phenomenon she has candidly discussed and deplored in recent articles, is held against her by some. She is the favorite target of a few columnists, notably Westbrook Pegler, who refers to her as "the widow" and blames her as the matriarch of the lively Roosevelt tribe for all the shortcomings of her relatives, living and dead.

Mrs. Roosevelt had no intention of remaining in public life after FDR died on April 12, 1945. On the contrary, she said then—and she has repeated frequently since—that she would like to slow down her life to a more leisurely pace, one befitting a woman with seventeen grandchildren and a great-grandchild. "After all," she declared only last week, "I'm an old lady. Why, I'll be 65 this fall."

Nevertheless, living on the Hyde Park estate in a sprawling twelve-room stone house, Val-Kill cottage—which for many years was a furniture factory—she is now even more active than she was in the White House. Probably the main reason is that she doesn't know how to slow down. Like all

the Roosevelts and the Halls (her mother's family), she has boundless energy.

She starts the day at full speed by bounding up, turning over her mattress, and making her bed. And she never lets up until she retires at night. Even when she is walking her Scotties, the famous Fala who is now nine and his grandson Tamas McFala, she tears across the countryside as though she were trying to catch a train. Just a shade under six feet, she strides like a man.

She appears to be in perfect health. The only infirmity of age she shows is a slight deafness in her right ear; she prefers visitors to sit on her left. Her hair is still soft and blond; her complexion is still fresh. The two prominent front teeth, in which the nation's cartoonists used to delight, were broken in an automobile accident three years ago; the porcelain caps replacing them are far more becoming.

The reason that Mrs. Roosevelt herself gives for continuing her activities is that "there is so much that needs doing." . . .

Mrs. Roosevelt's major interest . . . is the United Nations. She is a member of the American delegation, and chairman of the UN Commission on Human Rights. It is a backbreaking job, for she must often attend as many as three conferences a day.

At the UN, Mrs. Roosevelt has been personally popular with the Russians and with the delegates from Russia's satellites—but she has also infuriated them. The Communists recognize that Mrs. Roosevelt has influence even with their own people. What she says in defense of American Democracy and the American way of life—and in criticism of Soviet totalitarianism—carries enormous weight, for she is looked upon everywhere in Europe and Asia as a defender of "the common man."

For precisely that reason, when the State Department is particularly anxious to answer a Russian propaganda offensive, it calls on Mrs. Roosevelt. In recent years, the department has developed a great respect for her. Secretary of State Dean Acheson values her opinions highly and frequently consults her. . . .

Mrs. Roosevelt puts on a deceptively mild manner in answering the Communists. As she herself says, "I rarely give way to righteous indignation, and when I do it's not because I am angry; I do it for effect." She admits the United States isn't perfect, but she points out that Americans are perfectly aware of their country's faults, discuss them freely, and try to do something about them.

Then she wonders why she never hears the Communists confess that Russia and the satellite countries are not without blemish. Can it be, she asks, that the Communists don't recognize their faults? Or are they afraid of free discussion? Her words are silken, but the silk sheathes cold steel. . . .

Mrs. Roosevelt has faith in the UN. "You have to have faith," she asserts. "If you abandon hope for the world, what's the use of living?" Moreover, she is convinced that the Russians eventually will change their foreign policy. Russia's present intransigeance, she believes, springs from a conviction that capitalism is doomed, that world revolution is inevitable and imminent, and that Communism will soon triumph everywhere.

The Russians will do business with the United States only when they become convinced that we're in business to stay, in spite of Marx, Engles, and Lenin, Mrs. Roosevelt says. They're already beginning to have doubts about the "coming capitalist collapse," and if the United States remains economically stable and politically democratic, those doubts will eventually harden into a change of policy. "Meanwhile, we must remain firm with the Russians. The Soviets look upon compromise as evidence of weakness rather than as a gesture of good will." . . .

Despite her keen interest in the UN, Mrs. Roosevelt has on several occasions offered to resign from the United States delegation. Each time, Mr. Truman has refused to even consider the idea, laughing it off as preposterous. Mrs. Roosevelt is serious about quitting, however. She thinks "the United States should have a younger woman in the job."

The end of World War II brought peace, but also added the devastating power of nuclear weapons to the world's arsenal. ER, always a pragmatic pacifist, understood that the stakes in international relations were higher than ever. Like her husband, she believed passionately in the United Nations and went to great lengths to offer the world body her support. RIGHT: ER leads a discussion during a United Nations seminar at the Roosevelt home in Hyde Park, New York. Photo United Nations, courtesy National Archives

The women of the world found inspiration in Eleanor Roosevelt—across language and cultural barriers she symbolized to them the potential of all women to make a difference in their world. *LEFT: ER chats with a group of women during her visit to Delhi, India, in March of 1952.* Photo courtesy Franklin D. Roosevelt Library

The relationship between Eleanor Roosevelt and Winston Churchill was long and complicated. Churchill recognized ER's popularity and her influence on the citizens of the United States and his own country; a traditionalist when it came to women's place in public life, however, he was never totally at ease with her outspoken manner and independence. ER thought Churchill too wedded to the idea of the monarchy and not a staunch enough supporter of democracy worldwide, yet she also understood that his strength and leadership had seen the British people through the trials of World War II. *LEFT: ER and Churchill in London in 1948.* Photo by Bettman Archive

The last official public office held by Eleanor Roosevelt was that of chairperson of President John F. Kennedy's Commission on the Status of Women. ER was slow to give her support to candidate Kennedy, but once he was in office she came to see that he represented the future of some of the very ideas about equal rights and social activism she had worked a lifetime to promote. *RIGHT: ER with presidential candidate John F. Kennedy in October of 1960.* Photo by New York Post

The comfortable informality of ER's Val-Kill home was in sharp and deliberate contrast to the atmosphere of Springwood, FDR's boyhood home. Springwood's formal living room reflected Sara's reluctance to completely accept her daughter-in-law as part of the family: there were two matching armchairs—one for Sara and one for Franklin, with no accommodations made for ER. RIGHT: ER's living room at Val-Kill. Photo courtesy Franklin D. Roosevelt Library

"The people I love," wrote Eleanor Roosevelt in the years after leaving the White House, "mean more to me than all the public things." ER's five children—Anna, James, Elliott, Franklin, and John—were born during her twenties and early thirties when she was still struggling to emerge from the shadow of her mother-in-law, Sara Delano Roosevelt. By the time she had grandchildren, however, ER had the time, the confidence, and the perspective to simply enjoy their childhood. LEFT: ER with some of her grown children and grandchildren in May of 1950. Photo courtesy Franklin D. Roosevelt Library

For a woman who spent so much time on the road, ER had an amazing impatience with travel; she found trains and boats an exasperating waste of time and much preferred driving her own car (much to the dismay of her security personnel) and, above all, flying. At a time when air travel was still considered unsafe by many Americans—the president himself had a terrible fear of flying—ER took to the air without a second thought. In fact, so taken was she with flying that she began lessons with the pilot Amelia Earhart. The first lady eventually gave up her lessons in deference to the president's concerns for her safety, but she always spoke admiringly of women in flight and expressed regret later in life that she did not complete her own pilot training. RIGHT: ER carries her own bag to a plane at New York's LaGuardia Airport in 1960. Photo courtesy Franklin D. Roosevelt Library

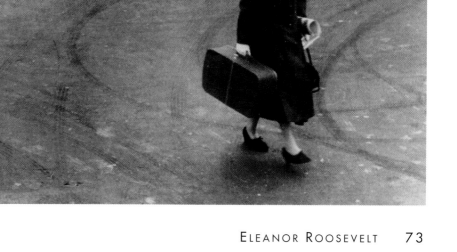

A LEGEND IN HER LIFETIME

BY HELEN GAHAGAN DOUGLAS

At a memorial service for Eleanor Roosevelt in 1962, Adlai Stevenson referred to her with the question, "What other single human being has touched and transformed the existence of so many?" His listeners were hard pressed for an answer. As first lady and as delegate to the United Nations, ER provided practical assistance and powerful inspiration for people across the globe and across the barriers of culture, language, and race. After her husband's death, ER spoke frequently of a time when she would retire to a quiet, private life; but she found there was always a cause worthy of her attention. Until her death she remained a prominent voice for peace and human rights. LEFT: ER with FDR's beloved Fala in 1948. Photo courtesy Franklin D. Roosevelt Library

Eleanor Roosevelt became a legend in her lifetime. Photographs convey only a part of her substance. They are a reminder of the gentle woman who exerted such unexpected and enduring force. They recall the scope of her activities and interests. They contribute to the legend, but they do not explain it.

Future generations will want to know what kind of woman Eleanor Roosevelt was. What was she like, they will ask. I was one who enjoyed her friendship—a friendship that affected the course of my life.

The Eleanor Roosevelt I shall always remember was a woman of tenderness and deep sympathy, a woman with the most exquisite manners of anyone I have ever known—one who did what she was called upon to do with complete devotion and rare charm.

The first time I met Mrs. Roosevelt was in 1929 at a benefit luncheon in New York City. I had been invited because I was a star in the theater. Mrs. Roosevelt was attending the luncheon as the wife of the Governor of New York. She was a plain woman, very tall, very thin, gracious, friendly; we spoke a few words. That's all I remember of that first meeting, except that I was told that the Governor's wife was interested in all kinds of welfare work.

I didn't know that she was already a most remarkable woman. At the time, her comings and goings were rarely recorded. Besides, I was very young and completely involved in my own career and not at all interested in governors' wives and their doings—or politics.

How could I have imagined, at that first meeting, that this unassuming, utterly unpretentious woman would become the most loved, the most cherished of First Ladies? That she would be trusted at home and in faraway lands by men and women who had never seen her, but knew they knew her?

Who could imagine that her influence and popularity would continue to grow even after the death of her husband, that her voice in national and international affairs would be given the utmost respect, that for sixteen years

"She walked in the slums and ghettos of the world," eulogized Adlai Stevenson, "not on a tour of inspection . . . but as one who could not feel contentment when others were hungry." For Stevenson, a close friend of the former first lady, and for countless others, this was ER's greatest gift to the world: her sense of true empathy. Although she was born into a life of wealth and privilege, ER always displayed an innate ability to understand the trials and suffering of others. LEFT: ER and a young girl at a milk bottling plant outside Washington. Photo by New York Times Photos

visiting dignitaries would seek her out as second in importance only to the President of the United States?

Who could imagine that this woman, who battled to overcome shyness, would travel the earth as though driven to do so by her need to see, to know, to understand people? Who could imagine that this shy woman would help to make the world small?

Who could imagine that the girl who thought of herself as plain would become a woman with more admirers than any of the famed beauties of history?

HER EXTRAORDINARY PERSONALITY

BY ADLAI E. STEVENSON

Eleanor Roosevelt lived an unprecedented life. Born into an insular, upper-class society that expected conformity and quiet dependence from its daughters, wives, and mothers, ER chose a different path and let an open mind, a generous heart, and an independent spirit guide her. RIGHT: ER as a young woman. Photo by Stock Montage

do not think it amiss to suggest that the UN is, in no small way a memorial to her [Eleanor Roosevelt] and to her aspirations. To it she gave the last fifteen years of her restless life. She breathed life into this organization.

The UN has meaning and hope for millions, thanks to her labors, her love, no less than to her ideals—ideals that made her, only weeks after Franklin Roosevelt's death, put aside all thoughts of peace and quiet after the tumult of their lives, to serve as one of this nation's delegates to the first regular session of the General Assembly. Her duty then—as always—was to the living, to the world, to peace.

My country mourns her, and I know that all in this Assembly mourn with us. But even as we do, the sadness we share is enlivened by her faith in her fellow man and his future which filled the heart of this strong and gentle woman.

She imparted this faith, not only to those who shared the privilege of knowing her and of working by her side, but to countless men, women, and children in every part of the world who loved her even as she loved them.

For she embodied the vision and the will to achieve a world in which all men can walk in peace and dignity. And to this goal, a better life, she dedicated her tireless energy and the strange strength of her extraordinary personality.

From a memorial speech to the United Nations following Eleanor Roosevelt's death in 1962.

Eleanor Roosevelt died on November 7, 1962, at her home in New York City. She was seventy-eight years old. Her funeral at Hyde Park was attended by President Kennedy and First Lady Jacqueline Kennedy, Harry and Bess Truman, Lyndon and Lady Bird Johnson, and Dwight Eisenhower. After the service, ER was laid to rest on the grounds of the Hyde Park estate alongside her husband. RIGHT: ER arrives in London in 1942 to study British women's part in the war effort. She is carrying a copy of Abraham Lincoln and the Fifth Column. *Photo courtesy National Archives*

FURTHER READING

Anthony, Carl Sferrazza. *The First Ladies*. Quill (William Morrow), 1991. This book tells the story of the evolution of the role of first lady, from the era of Martha Washington to that of Barbara Bush. A chronological presentation interweaves the lives of the first ladies with the history of the United States and describes how each individual woman shaped the demanding role to reflect her personality, her vision, and her times.

Cook, Blanche Wiesen. *Eleanor Roosevelt, Volume I*. Viking, 1992. The first of two planned volumes, this biography tells the story of ER's life from childhood to 1933, the year she became first lady, and provides a detailed account of ER's family, her education and upbringing, and the growth of her political involvement in the 1920s.

Douglas, Helen Gahagan. *The Eleanor Roosevelt We Remember*. Hill and Wang, 1963. A tribute to the former first lady in photographs accompanied by the words of some of her many admirers.

The First Ladies of the White House, Ideals Publications Incorporated, 1995. A companion to the book, *Our Presidents*, this volume includes a biography of each of the first ladies from Martha Washington to Hillary Clinton and is illustrated with formal portraits as well as photographs.

Goodwin, Doris Kearns. *No Ordinary Time*. Simon and Schuster, 1994. This Pulitzer Prize winning book tells the story of Eleanor and Franklin Roosevelt during World War II. It is a richly detailed history of wartime America, as well as a fascinating portrayal of the unique partnership between ER and FDR during their years in the White House.

Hoff-Wilson, Joan and Marjorie Lightman, editors. *Without Precedent: The Life and Career of Eleanor Roosevelt*. Indiana University Press, 1984. A collection of essays on the life, political career, influence, and legacy of ER.

Lash, Joseph. *Eleanor and Franklin*. Norton, 1971. In this Pulitzer Prize winning work of biography, Lash, a close friend of Eleanor Roosevelt, creates a portrait of both Eleanor and Franklin and tells the story of their relationship from their courtship through their years as president and first lady.

Lash, Joseph. *Eleanor: The Years Alone*. Norton, 1972. An account by ER's longtime friend Joseph Lash of the former first lady's active life in public service after the death of FDR.

Lash, Joseph. *Life Was Meant to Be Lived: A Centenary Portrait of Eleanor Roosevelt*. Norton, 1984. Published in honor of the one hundredth anniversary of ER's birth, this book features over one hundred photographs, some never before published, along with a biographical narrative by Joseph Lash.

Lash, Joseph. *Love, Eleanor: Eleanor Roosevelt and Her Friends*. Doubleday, 1982. Editor Joseph Lash presents a selection of the letters written by ER to some of her closest friends, including Lorena Hickock, Earl Miller, Nancy Cook, and Marion Dickerman.

Roosevelt, Eleanor. *On My Own*. Harper, 1958. ER's own account of the years after the death of FDR, with detailed descriptions of her work on the United Nations and of her many travels.

Roosevelt, Eleanor. *This I Remember*. Harper, 1949. ER's remembrances of life in the White House during her twelve years as first lady.

Ward, Geoffrey. *A First Class Temperament: The Emergence of Franklin Roosevelt*. Harper and Row, 1989. The story of Franklin Roosevelt's youth, his battle with polio, his rise to the presidency, and his twelve years in the White House.

Franklin D. Roosevelt National Historic Site, Hyde Park, New York. Located north of New York City on the Hudson River near Poughkeepsie, the FDR National Historic Site includes FDR's presidential library as well as the family home, *Springwood,* where FDR and ER lived with FDR's mother, Sara Delano Roosevelt. The library is open for tours and for research. Donated by ER to the U.S. government soon after the president's death, Springwood contains original furnishings as well as official and personal papers of the Roosevelt family. FDR and ER are buried on the grounds of the Hyde Park estate. Nearby is ER's *Val-Kill* cottage, which sits on 172 acres. Tours of Val-Kill focus on the life and achievements of Eleanor Roosevelt and feature a film biography, *First Lady of the World.* Admission is charged at both sites. The library is open year round; Val-Kill from March through October. Call for details on all three sites, (914) 229-9115.

The Library of Congress, 10 First Street, Washington, D.C. The largest library in the world, the Library of Congress holds millions of books, manuscripts, documents, photographs, and prints. Researchers looking to further their knowledge on the life of Eleanor Roosevelt will find a number of items relating to FDR's administrations and ER's years as first lady. The library is open to the public seven days a week. (202) 707-5000.

The National Archives, College Park, Maryland. The National Archives houses a massive number of photographs and documents of historical interest, including a particularly large collection from the World War II era. The Archives is open to the public for study and research. Call for information on hours and fees, (301) 713-6660.

Roosevelt Campobello International Park, Campobello Island, New Brunswick, Canada. The American and Canadian governments join in a unique partnership to fund this historic site, which includes the restored summer home of the Roosevelt family. The home is maintained as a museum in honor of FDR and his family, and it was the setting for the film *Sunrise at Campobello.* Housed here is a collection of family papers and memorabilia. The site is open to the public daily from late May to mid-October. Call (506) 752-2922 for more detailed information.

United Nations Headquarters, New York, New York. ER hoped to locate the United Nations headquarters at Hyde Park, but the more neutral site of New York City was eventually chosen. Tours of the building on 1st Avenue between 42nd and 48th streets are available, as are tickets to sessions of the General Assembly. (212) 963-7713.

The White House, 1600 Pennsylvania Avenue, Washington, D.C. Although with her busy schedule she was more often on the road than in residence, ER called the White House home from 1933 until 1945. Tours of the presidents' historic home are available, and admission is free. Call (202) 456-7041 for details.

I N D E X